Happy
R.A.V.I.N.G.
⌃Customers!

Six Powerful Steps to Grow Your Business
with Exceptional Customer Experience

D1456180

Carol Buehrens

Praise for Happy R.A.V.I.N.G. Customers!

"WOW! Just read *Happy R.A.V.I.N.G. Customers!* and Carol Buehrens 'gets it'. The statement that Customer Experience is a strategy, not a project is spot on. Any Company who really knows that Customer Experience drives profit must read this book. And, if you know a Company who doesn't get it, then they really need to read and embrace the R.A.V.I.N.G. approach."

> – Teresa Laraba, Senior Vice President Customers, Southwest Airlines

"*Happy R.A.V.I.N.G. Customers!* resonated with me, as it outlines very similar strategies that we use at Safelite AutoGlass to build a customer-driven culture. Carol provides practical advice that will help businesses, and their people, provide a memorable customer experience… and grow their bottom line. Since following similar tactics, we've doubled our business! Carol's toolkit breaks down what can feel like an overwhelming effort into actionable, real-world steps."

> – Tom Feeney, President & CEO, Safelite AutoGlass®

"Happy Raving Customers is a hands-on, user friendly book about delighting your customers. It provides a simple process for anyone to get started with this important work, with great real-time examples, tools, templates, and checklists that can be used easily. The book explains the importance of employees in delivering a great customer experience, as well as ways to foster a culture of continuous improvement and innovation. A must read for anyone interested in building a customer experience strategy as a competitive differentiator."

> – Karyn Furstman, VP Agent & Customer Experience, Safeco Insurance

"Businesses can no longer rely on simply building products – they must cultivate thoughtful and engaging experiences. In her 6-step process, Carol Buehrens deftly outlines a clear framework that, when followed, will transform ranting customers into raving fans."

> – Rob Scruggs, Director, Customer Experience, E*TRADE Financial

"*Happy R.A.V.I.N.G. Customers!* is a great read for anyone in business today. The book is divided into easy to consume chapters that explain practical steps to creating a customer-centric culture. Best of all, the book is like your own personal cheerleader to help you stay focused on innovating around great customer experiences."

> – Sharon Carmichael, Manager, Customer Insights & Analytics
> Sony Electronics

"Carol gets that it takes building a bond with customers to grow your business. Use her book to get handy tools and techniques for advancing yours with your customers."

> – Jeanne Bliss, President, CustomerBLISS, Author of *Chief Customer Officer*
> Cofounder, Customer Experience Professionals Association

"*Happy RAVING Customers!* is a book that everyone who wants to succeed in business must read. We all know that organizations that delight their customers outperform their peers. *Happy RAVING Customers!* is for everyone building a customer-focused business or refocusing an existing business on the experience of the customer. This is a book for the true Experience Makers who drive great customer experiences."

> – Sean Van Tyne, Director, User Experience, FICO
> Speaker and Coauthor of *The Customer Experience Revolution*

"The message in *Happy R.A.V.I.N.G. Customers!* speaks to everyone. Carol has done a wonderful job of creating tools and a message that can enable everyone in the organization to get on the same page."

> – Jim Rembach, Principal, Beyond Morale

"Join customer expert Carol Buehrens as she leads you through the customer experience journey in the excellent 'Happy R.A.V.I.N.G. Customers!'. Today, customers are much more than just the buyers of the stuff you market and sell; they demand exceptional experiences from their brands of choice. To deliver, you must deeply connect and understand them like never before. Carol lays out a simple six-step formula for every business that wants to serve…and thrive…by truly loving their customers."
   – Chuck Wall, Speaker, Entrepreneur and Author of Customer CEO: How to Profit from the Power of Your Customers

"*Happy R.A.V.I.N.G. Customers!* is a great pragmatic approach to helping elevate the way your organization approaches their customer centric initiatives. In this easy to consume guide you will come away with a new sense of drive to improve your customer experience processes. It highlights the need to focus every project, meeting, discussion, etc. on your customer experience strategy."
   – Tom Wolfe, Customer Experience ASM, Oracle

"I use *Happy R.A.V.I.N.G. Customers!* in the course I teach on 'Selling Customer Experience and User-Centered Design to Management' at California State University Fullerton. It's the best resource I've seen on the subject! As part of a graduate-level certificate program, the students are experienced professionals who want practical guidance they can use tomorrow to create change on their jobs. They love this book. You will too."
   – Joely Gardner, PhD, President, Human Factors Research, Inc.
   Adjunct Professor, California State University Fullerton

"Want a thriving business? Then happy customers are not enough. You need customers that stand up and rave about you. Carol Buehrens uncovers the six vital steps on the journey to winning RAVING customers. Packed with both insights and tools, *Happy R.A.V.I.N.G. Customers!* is a must read."
   – Stan Phelps, Chief Experience Architect, 9 INCH Marketing
   Author of *What's Your Purple Goldfish?* and *What's Your Green Goldfish?*

"*Happy R.A.V.I.N.G. Customers!* is an insightful resource for those creating business strategy as well as implementing it, from Customer Experience Innovation Award winner Carol Buehrens. This guidebook is part of 'the new marketing leadership' that begins with personas and customer experience journey mapping, and delivers invaluable customer experiences.

Companies considered 'customer experience leaders' are recognized as being better, different, more sustainable and profitable than most businesses. The expertise Carol shares in this book will help your business effectively begin the transition, from inside-out and outside-in, to become a customer experience leader The toolkit, by itself, is an invaluable facilitator for many of the steps critical for this transition. *Happy R.A.V.I.N.G. Customers!* is an essential addition to your go-to customer experience resources!"

– Jeofrey Bean, Principal, Del Mar Research
Speaker and Coauthor of *The Customer Experience Revolution*

"One of the biggest challenges companies have is integrating customer experience management within their culture, strategy, and daily activities – and involving all levels of employees, both front-line and 'far-line', as Carol puts it. This book shows you how to do that. I'd love it if every company I buy from would adopt the six R.A.V.I.N.G. steps!"

– Lynn Hunsaker, Customer Experience Optimization Strategist
ClearAction LLC

To view the full list of comments and reviews, visit
www.happyRAVINGcustomers.com/reviews

#happyRAVINGcustomers

You can follow Happy R.A.V.I.N.G. Customers! news using the hashtag #happyRAVINGcustomers on social media networks. Follow the author using @carolbuehrens.

Today's customers are changing their expectations at a rapid rate, so this book is updated as often as possible.

To view available updates, visit
www.happyRAVINGcustomers.com/updates

Published by MCH Press, www.mchpress.com

Happy R.A.V.I.N.G. Customers!
Six Powerful Steps to Grow Your Business with Exceptional Customer Experience
Carol Buehrens

This book is available in grayscale, full color and ebook formats.

Published in the United States by MCH Press
ISBN 978-0-9910274-0-8

Grayscale
FIRST EDITION

About the Author

Carol Buehrens has been constructing extraordinary customer experiences for over 30 years for major companies such as Liberty Mutual, Northrop, McDonnell-Douglas, Bechtel, General Electric, Mercury Marine, and ICW Group Insurance Companies.

Carol's passion for improving customer experience has resulted in numerous awards, including the prestigious "2012 CX Innovation Award" from the Customer Experience Professionals Association, ICW Group CEO Award, and the Liberty Mutual Star Award.

A Founding Member and Expert Panel Member of the international Customer Experience Professional Association, Carol is also a Board Member of the San Diego Software Industry Council's User Experience Business Interest Group, Expert Reviewer of the San Diego Customer Experience Special Interest Group, and Adjunct Professor at California State University Fullerton.

Also by Carol Buehrens

Adam and the Magic Marble
DataCAD for the Architect
DataCAD for Architects and Designers
VersaCAD Tutorial, A Practical Approach to Computer-aided Design
VersaCAD on the Mac

Contents

Preface

Customers are taking over the world today. They're demanding exactly what they want and are putting up with absolutely nothing less. To be successful, you've got to provide amazing customer experiences and you must act quickly. With the right process and tools at your fingertips, you can and will develop *Happy R.A.V.I.N.G. Customers.*

This book is written to provide you tangible and actionable steps, as well as a complete toolkit, to jump-start you on the road to success.

Let's start off with two stories. The first is about the importance of providing an *excellent customer experience*. The second is about the importance of nurturing a *customer experience culture.*

Are your customers held hostage?

I selected this story because it's a good illustration from a top executive who "gets it". He had been asked to deliver a keynote presentation to a new committee formed to help improve their company's customer services. The twelve committee members listened intently as the executive presented his rather long message. He suddenly stopped and said, "Look, I can talk until I'm blue in the face about the importance of a great customer experience. But let me tell you a story that just happened to me a few days ago." He then proceeded to convey an experience he and his wife endured while visiting their cellphone service provider's store to ask about a discrepancy with their bill.

"During this visit", he explained, "the young man who served us was less than helpful. He spoke to us curtly, looked disinterested, and then, without regard to completing our conversation, rudely moved on to assist another customer. He didn't resolve our issue, didn't provide friendly service, and, in fact, left us hanging mid-sentence as we were describing our issue."

The executive continued relating several similar encounters with the support line. "We'd leave them today, but we're being 'held hostage' against our will. Our email, Internet access, television cable, and landline are all tied to this same company, we've only been with them for 6 months and we're in a 2-year contract."

They were disgruntled customers with no easy means of escape.

He concluded his story, "We've told everyone – our friends, our relatives, our neighbors, and anyone else who would listen. And, now I've told you. *How does that make you feel?*"

By this point, everyone in the meeting felt his pain and resounded that they would never do business with that provider.

This, of course, was his point. Bad experiences and poor services lead to frustrated, disloyal customers *who tell everybody about their unhappiness.* They become your "ranting" customers. Their poor portrayal of your company affects future and current customers, and ultimately, your brand image. To have, grow and maintain loyal customers, you need to provide excellent services and experiences. And, to execute this effectively, you must listen to your customers, understand their pain and make a positive impact on their lives.

Have you ever been held hostage by a company? Have you ever been treated poorly as a customer and given no options to correct the situation? Wouldn't it be great if that company had listened to you, really listened, and improved the experience you were having?

From customer hat to helmet

There are so many examples about the need for a customer experience culture, it was hard to pick just one. I decided on the following story because it wraps up the sentiment of all of the others into a nice, neat bundle. And, quite frankly, it made me crazy.

I met with a project team to discuss a new Point of Sale system for their company website. Their current system was simple, easy to use, and they had received great feedback from the customers who used it. They were replacing it because the new system would greatly improve their *inside processes*.

During the meeting, my job was to represent the customers, which I refer to as "wearing my customer hat". In that vein, I had to deliver some tough news; during testing, the new system failed on several points. Many usability issues had been identified, ranging from labeling inconsistencies, an abundance of screens and redundant steps, an overly complicated and unreliable search routine, to an unusually high occurrence of errors that halted the checkout process.

It came as a complete surprise to me when the business stakeholders (the internal team who benefited from the automation of the new system), said they already knew about these issues! They had decided to continue with the rollout in spite of the poor experience the system provided. They insisted that it was a "wonderful application". They lovingly described their improved *internal process flow* as though it could stop world hunger. I argued that it wasn't ready for prime-time.

We were at an impasse – me, alone on one side representing the customer, and everyone else on the other side, representing, quite frankly, themselves.

I had entered this meeting wearing my soft, fuzzy customer hat, advocating for our beloved customers. I soon found that I had to exchange this hat for a helmet, because I was hitting my head against a brick wall!

The usage difficulties and errors made this decision a no-brainer for me; it stood in the way of customers (hint, "profit") and the team needed to roll up their sleeves and fix it. However, to the stakeholders, the efficiency it provided them made it worth any trouble their customers would suffer, hands down. To my horror, they even suggested including a tutorial describing workarounds for each issue and determined that the 20% error rate was an *acceptable cost of doing business.*

This may sound totally ludicrous to you. Would you feel comfortable launching a system like this that could negatively impact your bottom line? What would your customers say, think, do? So, what's going on here? If your head is spinning, let's just say that mine was ready to explode. Everyone in that room stood *against* the customer. From their viewpoint, the new system was "good enough" to roll out and customers would "be happy" using it simply because the internal stakeholders would have a better process.

Not an unusual situation

If you think this kind of attitude is rare, think again. When an organization's culture is NOT putting their customers first, NOT trying to make their customers successful, then this same scenario happens over and over again. This may be happening in project meetings throughout your own company.

If there's no focus on improving the experience for your customer, then it stands to reason the focus is on something else.

What's the focus at your company?

Steer your organization in the right direction – toward your customer. Follow this book's six easy steps. You'll find the philosophy and ideas presented make sense. They feel right. And they'll stand the test of time. Whether you're a strategist or practitioner, The R.A.V.I.N.G. Customer Toolkit will become an essential part of your portfolio. It's the secret ingredient you need to succeed.

When applying the R.A.V.I.N.G. Customer Process, you'll practice the art of customer experience design. Your goal – to set your company apart from the competition and thrust your business toward upward growth.

My goal is to help you succeed!

Introduction

Customers are much smarter today than you may think. They know which companies love them, honor them, respect them, and are trying to make them successful. Customers are loyal to these companies, they rave about them, they buy from them, and they recommend them to others. That's what this book is about – six steps you can take to create your own raving customers and devoted fans.

The discipline of managing "Customer Experience" is relatively new. Though you can find plenty of advice on the subject, the actual, practical steps to take and the tools to "get 'er done" are few and far between. Without a plan and process in place, the effort can seem overwhelming.

With this book, you'll be taken through each phase to begin to make this goal a reality at your own company. From the basic principles of strategic planning, to employing cultural change, this book holds your hand and provides the tools you need to be successful. Following the steps outlined in this book, along with The R.A.V.I.N.G. Customer Toolkit, your business can and will flourish, even in today's tough business climate.

What drives YOUR business?

The fact is that most businesses today are driven by the bottom line. As a result, they pay more attention to their profit margin than to their customers. That's sad when you think about it, because where would your business be without customers? You wouldn't have a business!

Let's face it, customers are your business. They drive it. Whether you sell toys or planes, are a B2C or B2B, it's hard to argue that if your customers stopped buying your products or services, you'd quickly be out of business!

Happy R.A.V.I.N.G. Customers! gives you the keys to make a difference between you and your competition.

To achieve raving customer status, you must provide more than products and services alone. You must offer exceptional experiences.

Do you offer great experiences?

Do you know the experiences your customers are having with your company? How can you find out? And, how do you begin to offer the great experiences needed to have customers rave about your company?

The answer is simple: Look at where you are, decide where you want to be, then put your heart, soul, blood, sweat and tears into getting there.

Of course, this means that "where you want to be" is all about your customers. It means that everything about your company is focused on this unifying vision. Your employees must concentrate their efforts on your customers, your products and services must align with making your customers successful, and everyone must work to improve the lives of your customers.

Happy R.A.V.I.N.G. Customers!

The title of this book says it all. You want more than just "happy" customers – you want customers who *rave* about your company. Having raving customers is a powerful concept. They act as your marketing agents, positively directing new customers your way. By employing

the R.A.V.I.N.G. Customer Process, you're following the right path to developing *"happy raving customers"*.

Use this book to differentiate yourself

It's a great privilege for me to be able to offer you the insights, tools, and advice in this book. I hope you find the six-step "R.A.V.I.N.G. Customer Process," useful, practical, and impactful. I hope it helps you think about what you and your employees do every day to positively affect the lives of your customers.

To grow your business, it stands to reason you should pay a lot of attention to your customers. You want happy, satisfied, and most importantly, returning customers that rave about your brand, so that you have a thriving business!

If you're craving customers, you must earn raving customers! So, read on and have fun applying the ideas provided.

Key takeaways

- Provide excellent customer experiences to develop raving customers.

- Raving customers help tell your story and sell your products.

- Employ the six-step "R.A.V.I.N.G. Customer Process" to develop your own *happy raving customers*.

Chapter 1

The Customer Experience Advantage

T he term "customer experience" is the latest buzzword everywhere you look. It's no wonder. After all, your customers are having experiences with your organization every day. They're comparing the experiences you offer with other companies just like yours. And, watch out, because your competition is fierce!

But, what does it all mean? The practice of customer experience, focusing on improving the experiences your customers have, isn't new. It's been around since the early ages. In fact, the oldest business known to man, and you know which one I mean, is totally, 100 percent dependent on its customer's experiences alone!

So, why all the recent buzz? Because, for years, most businesses have simply relied on providing good products and servicing their local

community. Due to their proximity, they held a captive audience. Before the age of the Internet, their customers were, more or less, dependent on the supply provided by these regional companies. But now, everything has changed.

Today, we live in a "consumer's market". More and more, customers are able to pick and choose where they buy their products. And which companies they decide to be loyal to. They're able to locate testimonials and recommendations online very quickly and easily, and are influenced by other consumers they've never even met.

As a result, the companies that have good products and services, accompanied by exceptional customer experiences, are winning!

Even with this flurry about customer experience, it's amazing how many businesses "just don't get it". They don't understand what this discipline is about. Or they lack the full support of their company and end up expending only a minimal effort. Perhaps they concentrate solely on their *customer service* department, failing to understand the *totality of the concept of customer experience*. Ultimately, they continue to fall back on poor decisions that aren't made on the behalf on their customer.

The great news is, this can be a wonderful advantage for you. With amazing customer experiences, you can outpace your competition and take the lead!

The customer experience definition

A high level definition of customer experience is the "cumulative impact of interactions your customers have with your company, people, services, and products." But, as a discipline, it's so much more.

It includes planning, managing, and designing experiences. You'll collect the voice of your customer by means of feedback, surveys, and more.

It means that you'll take action on issues you find negatively impacting experiences. And, it's a holistic, comprehensive approach to providing the best service and interactions possible for your customers. It also includes reshaping the culture of your workforce to focus on what matters most – your customers.

An advantage through a tough economy

Times are hard and over the past few years, even well-established companies have dropped like flies. But, look carefully at why these businesses have failed.

Even though there are several different scenarios, for the most part, these companies have misjudged their changing customers. Either they didn't keep up with what was needed, didn't provide it in the way it was wanted, or their competition stepped in to provide it more aligned to the needs of their evolving consumers.

The winners of the race, the surviving businesses, aren't crossing the finish line by accident.

They know that customer experience is the most important competitive edge in this new era.

The Netflix story

In 2010, you saw an established consumer giant, Blockbuster, defeated by a new uprising star, Netflix. The notable factor in this lesson is that these two rivals offered the *same, exact product*. They provided their customers with the same movies, in the same packaging, from exactly the same manufacturers.

The *only difference* was the customer experience. Netflix hit the sweet spot by understanding the transformations that their customers were going through. They paid attention to their evolving lifestyles and growing expectations. They put on their "customer hat" and worked to understand their customer's own viewpoints.

The customer experience Netflix provided gave them the *advantage to succeed.* And they wiped out their competition in the process.

The difference between customer experience and customer service

Great customer experiences come from companies where fantastic customer service is paramount. Yet, customer experience and customer service are two totally different disciplines.

While successful customer experience companies certainly have excellence in customer service at their core, customer service is most likely a fraction of your customer's total experiences with your company. (Unless, of course, customer service is the only product you offer, in which case it would be a majority.) In other words, customer service is one of many offerings that your customers experience, in a long chain of experiences, with your company.

In fact, customer service may be what you provide to help ease the pain of an otherwise poor customer experience! The reality is that, in many cases, your customer may not even experience customer service at all *if everything goes right.*

A phone system story...

A business acquaintance described a situation that many of us may be able to relate to, since we're all customers at some level ourselves. As a company with a growing customer base, they decided it was time to employ an automated phone system.

During the first month, while they were still working out the kinks with their new phone tree programming, many things went terribly wrong. Customers pressing the number for the support desk experienced long waits on hold. Calls were dropped. All too often, they were connected to the wrong extension. Many who hit "0" out of frustration found out there wasn't an operator. Most customers ended up being transferred several times before finding the correct person who could provide the help they needed.

The result were customers, who were already annoyed because they had experienced an issue and needed help, experienced additional irritations and exasperations. As a consequence, the support staff was saddled with much more to deal with than simply answering customer's questions. They dealt with enraged customers, who they first had to calm down before anything else. Only then could they proceed to help them with their original issue.

Fortunately, the support team was comprised of dedicated employees who went out of their way to provide excellent service, which saved numerous accounts!

In summary, customers *experienced* unnecessary frustration and irritation. Employees scrambled to provide these emotionally charged customers with the best customer *service* they could deliver during this difficult circumstance.

This demonstrates a great example of the difference between customer experience, which is an emotional model of the customer, and customer service, which is a reactionary model of the company.

Why is emotion so important?

Emotional responses act to "seal the deal" when it comes to all of our thoughts, reactions, and memories of experiences. It doesn't take a rocket scientist to know that, the higher our emotions are during an experience, the larger the impact it has on the way we recall the experience. For example, when you think back on a time that made you very angry, it's likely you'll become upset all over again, even if it happened years ago!

Interactions and events are combined and reinforced with emotions – thoughts, feelings, attitudes, opinions, and reactions, which help make up the memory of an experience. Plus, there's always some extra baggage; customers come to you with preconceptions and emotional images about your company. They already have their beliefs on what you should do for them. It's this entire emotional package and expectations that make the discipline of customer experience so complex and challenging.

Put simply, customer experience focuses on the customer and the collective impact – both emotional and practical – of their interactions with your organization.

Do you know how your customers "feel" when they...?

- See your ads

- Read your emails

- View marketing materials

- Visit your website

- Call your support line

- Talk to representatives

- Reference your manuals

- Use your products

- Try to resolve problems

- Read reviews

- Employ your services

- Open your product box

- Receive your bill

- Return a purchase

Customers are evolving... to be fickle

Today, more than ever, most consumers are likely to stop buying products from your company based on one poor experience alone. Put your "customer hat" on and think about a poor experience you had dealing with a company. What did you tell your friends and business associates? Possibly, you told them all about the situation and how much you disliked your experience. You may have even said that *you'd never deal with that company again*.

Just like you, great experiences make your customers feel good, happy, special and important. Bad experiences make them feel frustrated, upset, disappointed, and insignificant as a customer. It's that simple.

To top this off, technology has made it easier and faster for your customers to uproot their loyalties and find satisfaction elsewhere. Online, they can discover a wealth of reviews, testimonials, and recommendations. People are raving or ranting about their own experiences. Furthermore, they're eager to help your customers find your replacement.

Word on the street is your brand

Companies with great customer experiences have great brands. How they got there may not have happened the way you may think it did. These companies had a clear vision of what their brand represented. However, they didn't stop there. They took the *heart and soul of their brand directly to their customers.* They worked hard to provide their customers with the quality experiences needed to fulfill the promise of their brand value.

Your brand isn't about your own internal interpretation. It's not the fancy, brass plaque on your wall inscribed with your brand statement either.

Your brand, and its value, is defined by and through the experiences your customers have with your organization.

Your customers are undeniably your brand experts. They know much more than you do about your brand and experience it every day. They may have a very different viewpoint than yours – and *theirs is the one that counts!*

What's the word on the street about your brand? Does the "street cred" of your brand hold up and give you the competitive edge you're hoping it does? Do your customers know and love your brand? Do they RAVE about it?

Great employees foster raving customers

Your values are conveyed to the outside world through your employees. Be it through their voice, products, or the services they deliver. In actuality, your customer's experiences are the proof point of your brand. One way or another, your employees provide these experiences.

Without great employees supporting a great brand, you won't have raving customers. Start at the heart of your organization, your employees, so that you can provide exceptional experiences. Following the six-step R.A.V.I.N.G. Customer Process, you'll learn many ideas for growing your raving customer culture!

Sounds fantastic – how do I get it?

In order to achieve incredible customer experiences, it requires both discipline and disciples. You'll serve as your company's visionary as you follow the R.A.V.I.N.G. Customer Process. Your efforts will spread throughout your entire organization like wildfire. Disciples gathering around you will become customer advocates. Your endeavors may start small and influence only a few projects at first, and then grow to encompass all initiatives and mindsets.

To be victorious, you need a method that allows you to learn and improve, and then rinse and repeat. When you follow the R.A.V.I.N.G. Customer Process, you'll apply six powerful steps that are sustainable. You'll raise the bar on experiences you offer your customers and achieve a true *customer experience advantage.*

Key takeaways:

- The customer experience discipline focuses on the viewpoint and emotions of your customers.

- Today, more than ever, exceptional experiences are paramount to the success of your business.

- The true experts of your brand are your customers.

- Follow the R.A.V.I.N.G. Customer Process to develop raving, loyal customers.

Chapter 2

The
R.A.V.I.N.G.
Customer
Process

Like fans watching a ball game, your customers can quickly go from cheering to complaining. One minute they're up, the next they're down, depending on the players, the conditions, and the referee's minute-by-minute play decisions. In order to provide consistent experiences that are above the ordinary, it takes planning and hard work.

That's where the R.A.V.I.N.G. Customer Process comes in. Following this systematic approach will help you understand where your organization is today, where it needs to go tomorrow, and how to get there in order to gain raving customers.

Why would you want raving customers? The bottom line is that customers who rave about you mean far more to the growth and profitability of

your company than ordinary, satisfied customers. Raving customers are delighted consumers who share high opinions about their exceptional experiences with your company to all who will listen.

This concept isn't new. However, what is new is the ease at which the word, good or bad, can travel.

An online buying story

My daughter provided me with a good example of how rapidly a good experience can degrade, due to these types of "plays in motion" that are often inadvertently created by well-intentioned companies.

She received a brochure in the mail from a very popular and fashionable clothing manufacturer, and had eyed a pair of slacks that were on sale. The brochure included a coupon that could be used online for a greater

discount on all sale items. She showed me this great deal and encouraged me to buy something too, and sent messages to her friends. (RAVING Customer!)

She found the slacks on the website, added them to her cart, and happily began the checkout process, still encouraging me to purchase a pair for myself. (Still a raving customer!) She turned to the coupon and entered the "extra 40% off" purchase code.

At that point, to our surprise, the coupon was not accepted.

My daughter was now forced to troubleshoot the situation. She picked up her cellphone and leafed through her emails until she came upon the electronic version of the same coupon, and applied this code, but to no avail. She searched their website and found no clue as to why the coupon codes were ineffective. At my suggestion, she called customer service for help with the purchase.

She was told by the service representative, "Those slacks don't apply to the coupon. They aren't on sale."

"But it says they are 30% off the regular price. Isn't that a reduced item on sale?" she asked.

"Yes," the service representative told her, "they are discounted, but that isn't a sale. It's a special purchase. A special purchase isn't a sale, so the coupon doesn't apply. If the price ends in 68 cents, it means it's a 'special purchase'. If it ends in 99 cents, it's considered a reduction, or *on sale*."

Customers don't care about internal rules

It makes absolutely no sense that this company expected their customer to understand this bizarre pricing scheme. But, how many times have we expected our own customers to know an internal rule or process, or even our organizational structure? Customers shouldn't have to understand our inner workings! Nevertheless, this same thing happens time and time again, at almost all companies.

Rest assured that my daughter was on the phone until a manager approved the coupon (after all, she is my daughter). But, not until she invested 50 minutes of frustrating conversation with a customer representative, who was unwilling to understand and make a price correction.

The power of social media

During this phone call, I observed a much larger lesson we can all learn – *this wasn't the only conversation she was having during those 50 minutes!*

The entire time she was involved in this coupon fiasco, she was sending out messages on her cell (tweeting and texting), to her friends. Her thumbs were literally flying.

When she was put on hold, she had more time to focus on communicating her emotions. And, her friends were answering her back about their own poor experiences, advising her on what to do next.

She was no longer a raving customer, she was a RANTING customer. And, in case you aren't up on social media, to make this perfectly clear, when I stated she sent messages to her "friends", I don't mean her 4 or 5 girlfriends. A "friend" in today's world is anyone who she is "connected to", which probably totals well over 350 people. And, those individuals, as they reply back, might be communicating to their network of "friends" who build on top of this list, and so on.

The more people that get involved, the more the word spreads like wildfire. Which is why, in no time at all, thousands of people can be reading the rants started by a single, poor customer experience.

It stands to reason, then, that having raving customers is enormously important. Raving customers, those who are overtly loyal to your company are much more likely to forgive a single poor experience than a merely satisfied customer. When they send messages to their friends, they are lavish raves of joy!

RAVING Customers spread the great word about you to others: to friends, family, other customers, in reviews, on blogs, through social media – to anyone who will listen.

From rant to rave in 6 powerful steps

As in the previous story, if you don't actively review and manage your customers' experience, you may be encouraging ranting behavior. Instead, learn to earn the raves from your raving customers! Follow the The R.A.V.I.N.G. Customer Process and start on the road to creating your own WOW factor.

The following chapters explain the six steps of the R.A.V.I.N.G. Customer Process. From R to G, you'll be guided through each phase. You'll find a wealth of creative ideas that will help make the entire process easy for you to employ at your own company.

The 6-step R.A.V.I.N.G. Customer Process

R = **Reality check.** Take a step back and assess where you are today.

A = **Align with strategy.** Ingrain customer experience with strategic planning.

V = **Vote to change.** Take care of politics and get everyone pointed in the same direction, from the top down.

I = **Innovate in unexpected ways.** Raise the bar to create awesome, exceptional experiences.

N = **Note success.** Reward your employees and grow your customer-centric culture.

G = **Get feedback.** Listen, listen and keep listening to your customers!

Gain the raving customers competitive edge

You know the amazing customer experience brands – Apple, Amazon, Zappos, Starbucks, Disney, Virgin Atlantic, Lexus, Nordstrom, and the like. These are companies that are successful because they have not only made excellent customer experience their goal, they've gone above and well beyond. They've made growing raving customers their business and "providing the WOW factor" their hallmarks. These successful companies have made incredible customer experiences their differentiator. They've learned the secret to achieving raving customers – *and so can you!*

Mind-blowing customer experiences don't have to be a secret only available for the big brands. By following the R.A.V.I.N.G. Customer Process, YOUR company will grow your own raves.

Key takeaways:

- RAVING Customers spread the good word about your company.

- It takes awesome experiences to earn this type of loyalty.

- The R.A.V.I.N.G. Customer Process is a powerful approach to creating and growing your own raving customers!

Chapter 3

R = Reality Check

Before you do anything else, take a step back to assess where you are today when it comes to your customer's experiences. Taking a reality check will help you establish your starting point and will be foundational for the rest of the R.A.V.I.N.G. Customer Process. At the core of your reality check is to identify who your customers are, what they're experiencing, and the impact of your employee culture.

Who are YOUR customers?

Knowing your customers – who they are, their lifestyles, wants and needs – allows you to center your attention on them as you create experiences. Experiences mean different things to different people, and the best experiences are designed purposely for specific customers.

For example, when I have an experience, I'm looking for age-appropriate, trustful interactions that makes me feel valued for who I am. When my daughter has an experience, she is looking for stylish, modern experiences that make her feel important for the young, informed woman she is. When YOU have an experience, you may be looking for something completely different. Between the three of us, we may represent three different kinds of customers.

Because we're different people, with different ages, incomes, needs, and lifestyles, we expect different experiences.

Ideas for understanding your customer types

Ask employees – Many front-line employees will know various customer types from their interactions with them. Check for established and changing trends.

Ask business partners – This can be very helpful if you are in a B2B industry. Often, the final consumer is well known by your front line business.

Survey customers – Ask them specific questions to help type them, such as age, income, regional location, insightful interests, buying habits, etc.

Hold focus groups – Get groups of customers together to determine types and buying habits.

Segment by profitability – Once you know your customer types; further segment them into the most profitable for your business. You'll want to target those customers first.

Segment by experiences – Try to understand the experiences your customers have had prior to coming to your company. This will help you understand what they expect from you. Especially if those experiences were with your competitors.

Learn who your customers are

If you don't know everything about your customers, find out. Learning about your customers is foundational to everything else. Even if you begin by simply writing down your basic impressions about your customers, taking the first stab at this is much better than not having any information at all! As mentioned in the previous chart, grow your knowledge by asking employees in your company and your business partners. Conduct customer surveys. Interview customers.

Even if you think you know your customers already, they are constantly evolving, so check your data often.

Companies getting the largest slice of the pie are those who thoroughly understand their customers and are able to provide them with excellent, focused, specialized experiences.

B2B industries pose extra challenges

Some business, such as B2B industries (businesses selling to other businesses who then sell to consumers), may feel removed from their final consumer. This can make it hard to understand their ultimate consumer or to get that data. If this is your situation, you really have two customers – the businesses you sell to plus the ultimate consumer of your products.

This hierarchical, or multi-tiered, sales model provides you with even more opportunities to create great customer experiences! You need to understand both levels of customers, because your sales model depends on both.

The challenge is in discovering what each party needs to be a successful and satisfied customer!

Customers are more than buyers

When it comes to defining the word *customer*, be sure to broaden your view to include others who may not be "buyers of your products", yet still have an impact on your brand. These individuals know you in other ways and may influence your consumers. Examples include:

- Subscribers to your blogs and those connected to your company via social media networks,
- Those who correspond about your company, such industry reporters,
- Career seekers,
- Your competition,
- And most importantly, your employees.

An influencer is someone who sways others by issuing their own opinions about your company. Good or bad? It's up to you.

Got the data? Start archetyping!

Once you've gathered data about your customers, you may have found out that you have many, many customers. Potentially, these many customers could have many different expectations. But, as you can imagine, it's next to impossible to design customized experiences for every single individual. So what can you do?

You can make organization out of this chaos by "grouping" your customer data into several broad categories, types, traits, and patterns. These groups are referred to as "archetypes".

Through the use of archetypes, you can begin to get a handle on your targeted audiences. By clustering traits, you create hypothetical customer profiles. This allows you to focus on their experiences and emotions by drawing conclusions based on the information you know about them.

Many businesses use archetypes. Depending on their need, they may develop a few or create dozens to help represent their main customer

types. For example, a car company employs different archetypes for each model of car they offer. They develop several archetypes to represent levels and types of buyers. They may have:

- Entry-level, first-time buyers,
- Those who will spend more but want economy,
- Family-centric buyers,
- Buyers demanding ultimate, and pricey, elegance.

Add the human touch with personas

Once you've developed your archetypes, humanize them by creating personas. Add a face and personality to each by using the Customer Experience Persona Templates found in Chapter 10, "The R.A.V.I.N.G. Customer Toolkit". Also, be sure to check out Chapter 5, "V = Vote to Change", for more about personas and how this useful strategy helps your employees connect emotionally with your customers.

What are your customers doing?

Another vital part of your reality check is to discover what your customers are currently experiencing. Do you know every encounter your customers are having with your company, including what they read, hear, and see, through your website, marketing materials, representatives, support line, email, and snail mail correspondence?

Are your customers happy, or even satisfied, with each of their encounters with your company?

Years ago, it seemed as though we had our hands full worrying about letters, phone calls and an occasional face-to-face. *That seems so uncomplicated now!*

Business has become complicated and involves a multitude of ways customers can interact with you.

Today, this is just the tip of the iceberg. Now you need to worry about a whole host of "channels", including websites, event sites, microsites, landing pages, emails, applications, intranets, extranets, portals, blogs, marketing campaigns, online references, print materials, press releases, (take a deep breathe now because the list goes on), automated replies, customer support scripts, videos, webinars, social media, storefronts, face-

to-face, automated voice response systems, mobile apps, and more. The list, literally, grows every day with new interactions and technology.

Your customers interact with your organization via this variety of different channels, and you need to know what they're experiencing during these interactions. As mentioned in Chapter 1, *"Customer Experience is the cumulative impact of interactions – both emotional and practical – your customers have with your company, which includes people, services, and products."* Since the majority of experience is emotionally based, you also need to learn how each one of these interactions makes them "feel".

Sounds daunting? Let's take a deep breath and simplify it a little...

Each interaction is a touchpoint

Each time a customer interacts with your organization, it's a "point" of interaction, or where they "touch" your company. In customer experience terms, this is referred to as a "touchpoint". For example, a customer receives and reads an email you send as part of a marketing campaign. This email is a touchpoint.

Your customers move from one touchpoint of your company to the next. They click on a link in an email and go to your landing page, the next touchpoint. Now, on this landing page, your customers download a PDF, another touchpoint. From one touchpoint to the next, your customers experience your company. It's like a little trail – where they go next is up to you. Sometimes their trail is a very enjoyable hike. Their path is clearly marked, the slope is gentle, the trees are beautiful. Other times, the trail may be confusing, steep and dangerous.

The trail becomes a journey

Each of these touchpoints link together, one by one, to become a customer experience journey. You may have several journeys for your customers and focused journeys for your different customer types. Small businesses may have just a few journeys, and larger businesses may have dozens, more complex journeys.

Customer experience journey maps

Journey maps are strategic tools that gather all of the touchpoints into a comprehensive view. From this view, you can better understand what customers are experiencing, which will lead you to improvements of

experiences and touchpoints. To inspire raving customers, each journey should be delightful, cohesive, and a positive continuation of the overall experience with your brand.

Mapping journeys is a critical part of your reality check. See Chapter 10, "The R.A.V.I.N.G. Customer Toolkit", Journey Map Details, to assist you with collecting information about each step.

Your first journey map

Identify an initial journey you'll capture. As in the previous example, start with a small task to get your feet wet. It can be as simple as: "A new customer making their first purchase" and consist of 4 or 5 touchpoints.

Begin by capturing your employee's concept of the journey. This internal view will help you become familiar before interviewing your customers.

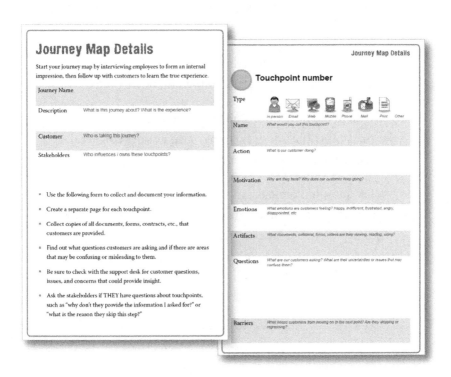

Initial touchpoint investigation

Ask the following questions to learn more about the journey
you're mapping.

- Who is the customer taking this journey?

- What is this touchpoint? Give the touchpoint a name, such
  as initial contact, registration, etc.

- What type of touchpoint is this? Email, phone call, website,
  in person, mobile app, online chat, document?

- What are customers expected to do at this point?

- What motivates them? Why are they at this step and why do
  they continue?

- What emotion are they feeling at this point? What have you
  heard? Are they happy, glad, indifferent, or frustrated?

- Are there documents or information customers see or use
  at this point? Include everything, such as sales collateral,
  forms, emails, videos, user manuals, web pages, etc.

- What questions are customers asking at this point? Are they
  calling the support line, sales representatives, others? Are
  they experiencing barriers, issues?

- Do they know what to do next?

Ask "stakeholders" (business leaders who own the various steps), and your front-line employees (those who work directly with customers). Get the right people involved at the very beginning – this is the team you'll want to celebrate with when the mapping is completed (and when, together, you make journey map improvements)!

Capture customers emotional plights

Emotions need to be documented as part of the journey. At each touchpoint, your customers experience real feelings. These ebb, flow, wax, wane, and most importantly, accumulate. Customers may feel happy at one touchpoint, and then, when the next touchpoint fails, they can become disappointed, frustrated or angry.

Remember, at this strategic level, your websites, applications and systems are mere touchpoints that you map and collect "experience details" on, such as how the customer felt overall about using the system, whether they had issues, stumbled into a roadblock, etc.

The good news – each one of these touchpoints is an opportunity to raise the bar and make customers feel wonderful about your company!

Note observations about touchpoints that reveal poor experiences. Those will be the ones you'll want to target for further analysis and improvements. At the same time, add big stars to ones that reveal great experiences. These are insightful events that provide you with information about what your customer's "like". Be sure to keep these and use the same ideas to improve other touchpoints!

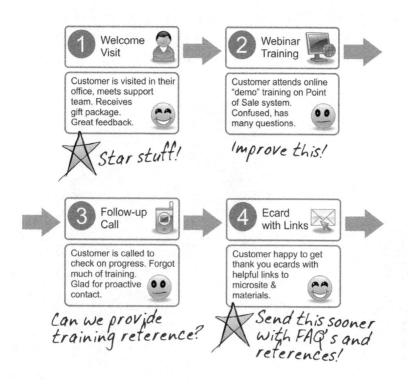

Creating a high-level journey map

Once the touchpoints are identified, you can create a high-level map. The goal is to help you gain an overall *"snapshot view"* that you can use to communicate to others what your customers are experiencing.

See Chapter 10, "The R.A.V.I.N.G. Customer Toolkit", High-Level Journey Map, for the helpful template to create an easy-to-understand, top-down view.

Your High-Level Journey Map is a powerful tool to use for project approval. Pass it around to others and gain feedback from stakeholders, managers, project teams, and front-line employees. Make certain that everyone agrees with this journey. Attain a consensus that the touchpoints are correct before continuing. (Don't be surprised when further touchpoints are revealed once additional eyes are on the journey.)

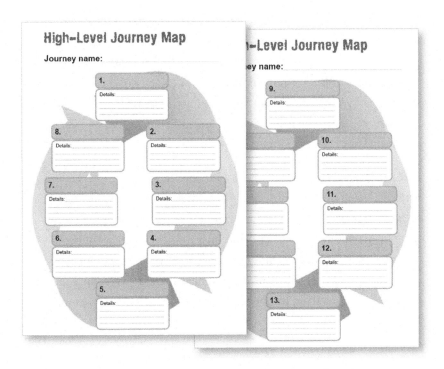

You may find gaps in your service, complicated points that can be streamlined or redundancy issues. Often this document, along with the detailed information you've collected, can be so revealing that you get immediate approval to make customer experience improvements!

The internal process trap

As you collect details, you may be pressured to add internal business process flows to your map. Resist this temptation! Customer experience journey maps are about your customers (hence the word "customer"). You're identifying what happens to *them*, not to your company.

If you add your internal processes to the same map, you'll lose the goal of the tool. You'll run the risk of any resulting project being focused on improving your own workflows, not centered on improving your customer's experiences.

This is not to say that your company shouldn't map and improve processes whenever possible! Often, improvements on internal workflows have a positive impact on customer's experiences, as well as result in a calculable "return on innovation" (more on that later in Chapter 6, "I = Innovate in Unexpected Ways"). This is just fair warning to *capture the internal process on another map*. Keep very clear goals for this strategic tool and the focus totally on your customers.

Like the Wizard of Oz, what happens behind the shiny green curtain is magic. What this means is, *customers really, really, really don't care about your internal processes*. They expect, and perhaps hope and pray, that you are taking great care of your business. They care about their own processes, workflows, time, and resources. They want to find your products easily, order them quickly, and have them delivered on time and at the quality agreed on. It's about "their experience" with your company.

Through the eyes of your customers

Be sure to follow up with steps to understand the journey through the eyes of your customers. After all, this is *their journey*. Talk to as many customers as possible to gain a better understanding of what is really happening at each touchpoint.

The only way you can get to the truth of what customers are experiencing is through your customers. And, quite often, it can be very different from what internal employees feel your customers *"should"* be experiencing.

As mentioned earlier, there are several ways to get this information, including interviews, surveys, and focus groups. Find out if your customers agree with the touchpoints you've collected. Most likely, you'll uncover additional points internal employees aren't aware of, especially those that cross departmental boundaries. You might learn that customers are skipping touchpoints employees felt were important. Get their pulse on each interaction – are they happy, informed, satisfied, confused, frustrated? Ask which touchpoints they feel are important and which ones are "show-stoppers". Learn what would make this experience a perfect "10"!

Put your customer hat on

During your reality check, try your best to see and understand through the *eyes of your customers*. As I said before, I refer to this as wearing your "customer hat".

Remember to put on your customer hat so that you can truly advocate for your customers. Work hard to teach others how to wear their own customer hats, too!

Your customer hat is one of the most important tools you have in your arsenal. Wear it proudly!

Are your employees customer-centric?

Having a customer-centric organization is paramount to being a superior customer experience company. Since all customer experiences begin in one form or another with your employees, they are at the heart of your reality check. Collectively, they make up the culture of your organization. From your top executives on down, your company and your brand are the total results of your employees.

What is their focus and drive? What motivates them? Do they connect and empathize with customers? Are their decisions based on the overall impact to customers? Would it be easy for them to put on their "customer hat"?

Get your ducks in a row with your inside customers first – your employees. Change their experiences, impressions, attitudes, and culture. This will set you up for future success.

Learn how to help your employees become customer focused, and find many ideas, in Chapter 5, "V = Vote to Change". Also, be sure to check out Chapter 7, "N = Note Success", for fun reinforcement strategies.

Survey your employees

Ask your employees the same questions you ask your customers. It's not unusual to learn employees have a totally different opinion from your customers. The results will assist you in pinpointing "gaps" and adjusting internal impressions.

Employees often misjudge the expectations and satisfaction levels of customers, as well as the importance of certain touchpoints.

There are many things to consider when doing your Reality Check. We've only scratched the surface on ideas to help you understand the current state of your customer experience. Once you've started on the R.A.V.I.N.G. Customer Process, you'll find many more opportunities for reality checking. *Just remember to keep the good stuff and earmark the rest for improvement!*

Key takeaways:

- Do your "reality check" first, so that you know what needs to improve.

- Learn as much as you can about your customers, in order to deliver experiences important to them.

- Identify all of your customer's journeys and touchpoints. These add up to their experiences with your company.

- Wear your customer hat to better understand the experience from their viewpoint.

- Find out if your employees are focusing on your customers.

Chapter 4

A = Align
with Strategy

O nce you've completed your reality check, the next step is to decide what you want to accomplish with your customer experience efforts.

Customer experience is a strategy, not a project or initiative. For your efforts to be effective, this ideal must exist in the strategic layer of your organization. Does your company already have a customer experience strategy? If not, you're not alone. However, in order to be a successful customer-centric company, one that focuses on developing raving customers, you'll need a strategic plan in place that ties in with your business strategy.

Ideally, your customer experience strategy will be fully woven into the fabric of your business strategy as a core component.

Planning an actionable strategy

Before formulating your strategy, think about the future of your company and what you wish to gain from improving your customer experiences. Where do you want your company to be in terms of customer experience in the next one, three, and five years. What about in ten years?

Once you've answered these questions, you can begin to formulate your strategy statement and plan. Priority is everything when planning, and you'll need to decide what you want to achieve first.

Do you want to...

- Increase your competitive edge?

- Grow your customer base or market share?

- Retain customers by building brand loyalty?

- Improve ease of doing business, so that it's easier to do business with you than with others?

- Add value to your company's brand?

- Improve and strengthen your brand image?

- Earn raving customer status?

Customer experience strategy statement

Be sure to create a strategy statement that is easily understood by your employees. This is not the time to be esoteric or vague. To truly innovate your company, your statement should contain a clear, concise, and actionable message to positively affect your end game. Keep in mind that only exceptional experiences will set you apart from your competition.

It's no longer good to be "good enough" when it comes to Customer Experience. You must have the WOW factor!

Employees need to know how the strategy impacts them, and how they, individually and together, impact your customers. You'll want it to:

- Capture your customer's success,
- Contain the service value of your brand,
- Be brief, repeatable and in everyday terms,
- Synergize employees to focus on your customers.

Creating a strategic plan

Your customer experience plan should deliver results. You'll want to better understand your customer, so you'll include research. You'll want your culture to be more customer focused, so you'll include your employees and the grooming of leadership in the customer experience discipline. To create awesome experiences, you'll need to take into account the restructuring of current experiences. You'll also want to include continuous measurement and feedback. Your plan should highlight the following:

- A shared vision across your organization,
- The needs of your target customers,
- Monitoring of interactions,
- Collecting and acting on customer feedback,
- Communications,
- Employee accountability,
- Celebration of successes.

Goals and objectives

A mainstay of your game plan will be the goals and objectives. Each goal should align with your strategy; the objectives should describe how the goal will be attained and measured for success.

Your goals and objectives may include such areas as:

- **Understanding your customer.** Employ customer research to identify customer segmentation, learn expectations and emotional attributes, regularly ask for feedback, and create advisory committees.

- **Becoming a more "customer-centric" organization.** Connect employees with customers, ingrain your customer into everything you do, employ customer personas for every project, and understand how decisions affect your customers.

- **Delivering emotionally engaging customer experiences.** Design experiences that delight the senses, look for new ways to surprise and delight customers at regular intervals in their journey, allow customer to help design the products they use.

- **Continually measure and improve.** Design systematic measurement techniques, employ regular measuring of experiences, continue to identify opportunities, track and communicate improvements.

- **Growing leadership.** Develop internal training, invite experts in to provide leadership presentations, identify helpful seminars and webinars, and encourage joining professional customer experience and customer service associations.

- **Driving cultural change.** Provide training, engage employees with customer-focused activities, create committees that forward customer-focused ideals, tie performance evaluations and merit increases with customer experience objectives, offer continuous communications, and celebrate successes.

Communicate, communicate, communicate!

After you make sure your plan is easy to understand and accomplish, communicate it to your entire employee population. This is a very important step. The problem is, many companies fail miserably at communicating. In fact, "lack of communication" is one of the top employee complaints in many organizations.

I recently attended a seminar about communications, where they cited 2 numbers you may find interesting.

87% and 19%

These numbers were from a large survey they had completed across several previous seminars. When the presenters were asked "how well they felt they communicated their topics", 87% responded they *"did a great job"*. But, when the audiences were asked the same question, *only 19% agreed!*

I'm a firm believer that there is no such thing as over-communicating. (If someone tells you that you over communicated, maybe it's because they finally got it!) Don't assume or downplay the art of communication – it should be an integral part of your plan. Consider pairing your communications with some sort of activity (contest, raffle, etc.), for a higher success rate. Lastly, plan succinct communications at regular intervals, perhaps once a month or even more often.

Ingraining the strategy

For your customer experience strategy to be successful, your employees need to hear it, get it, understand it, and *live it*. It needs to be a natural part of how they conduct their daily work routines. For example, if your strategy includes "achieve easy, intuitive customer experiences across all products and services", employees should task themselves daily to make that happen, at every possible occasion, without giving it a second thought.

Work with leaders and managers to identify ways to entrench this strategy into the everyday work life of your employees. Assign the task to one of your "employee committees" to help with this effort.

One company I worked with had a unique way to really get this point across at the project level. Since they used presentation slides to run project meetings, they added their customer experience strategy statement to the first page in their presentation template. On the subsequent page, project managers were asked a few questions to help describe how their project supported this strategy.

Each meeting started with the facilitator explaining just how their project "fit", how it was going to benefit their customers, and what they were doing to improve the overall experience.

Not only was the customer experience strategy reinforced, the dots were connected for the entire project team at every meeting.

Following this same idea, if your strategy included a statement about "achieving an easy, intuitive customer experience", you might have your project team members ask themselves:

- Are we doing all we can to make this an easy process?

- If we ask our customers, will they say this is easy to use?

- Is this new process easier than our competitor's?

- Is it as simple as A, B, C?

Look for other ideas to instill the strategy into your employees' daily work life. You could put it on posters, include it as part of your signature line in emails, mention it at every meeting, and have the president send out reminders. You could also create employee incentives, such as holding contests for ideas that strengthen the strategy, giving Customer Experience Awards, celebrating successful gains that align with the

strategy. The ideas are endless. Be sure to check Chapter 7. "N = Note Success", for additional and fun employee participation ideas!

In summary, create a strategy and plan that everyone can understand. Don't take it for granted that one communication will create the lasting impression you need to make your effort a success. Look for ways to reinforce and ingrain.

Make sure everyone hears it, understands it and practices it, again and again. Yell it, sing it, chant it!

Key takeaways:

- Decide what you want your future to look like, then create a customer experience strategy to get there.

- Be sure your plan contains the essential ingredients for success.

- Don't downplay communication and education. Be sure everyone knows and understands the strategy.

- Don't leave it to chance – ingrain your strategy into your organization.

Chapter 5

V = Vote to Change

This is so important, it stands repeating: To be a successful, *customer experience company*, your employees need to live and breathe your customer experience strategy.

But, without the right "votes", you won't get your strategy off the ground. Nothing will kill your efforts faster than neglecting to have the full buy-in from your top "Generals". Even if you've carefully assessed where you are (R = Reality check) and created a great strategy to follow (A = Align with strategy), you still need to take care of politics and get everyone pointed in same direction.

Start at the top

This is a top-down effort that has its core based in your business strategy. If your upper management and executives don't cast a "pro vote", your efforts are bound for failure.

Becoming a "customer experience excellence company", one with raving customers, requires the buy-in from the top. Just like your core business strategy, this is NOT a "bubble-up" proposition! As a strategic concept, the Generals need to vote for it, align and lead the army. From the president, CEO, vice presidents, and managers, to all employees – everyone in your organization must be marching in the same direction, to the same drummer.

Your leaders are the spearheads of this change. They must talk it, walk it, and breathe it. If this is their idea, and they own it, it will be a win for everyone. If you're the leader, then fantastic – you're already reading this book!

The vote = a cultural shift

Becoming a customer experience company and developing raving customers requires your entire organization. Getting everyone aligned in the same direction may be a huge change for your company. And, unless

you are one of the very few customer-centric organizations already, make no mistake – this will be a cultural shift for your employees. Change isn't easy. In fact, it can be downright scary.

To become a customer experience organization, all employees must be focused on the customer, provide great customer service, and have exceptional experiences designed and driven by customers.

The problem is that today, most employees are focused on themselves and the daily operations of the organization. This situation isn't by accident – it's been developed over time by design. In the past twenty years or so, most organizations have centered their attention on improving internal processes, reducing costs, and, most recently, continuing operations in spite of reductions in workforce.

As a result, much or all energy has been concentrated on efficiency of processes, increasing employee morale, and performance merits have been based on the bottom line – NOT on customer success!

Moving your organization's mindset in the other direction – to your customers – will not be easy. It's a tall order and your company's leaders will be your strongest guideposts to light the way. To develop raving customers, everyone in your company will need to vote to make the change; to be accountable to customers, for thinking of customers first, to offer excellent service, and for providing outstanding customer experiences.

Therefore, take the time required to attain the top political "vote". Get the buy-in and commitment needed, and you'll be happy you did.

The president and the printer

Challenged getting the top brass to vote for change? You may want to throw politics out the window, but here's an idea. To get past top-level political struggles, get them involved.

One company was having a problem with their CEO "walking the talk". He was providing lip service, but wasn't really backing the strategy. The team bravely decided to have him don his "customer hat" and go through what their customers were experiencing when installing one of their top selling printers.

The CEO eagerly accepted the challenge. That morning, a box arrived at his desk to begin his "experience". He opened it, took out the contents, and began following the instruction manual to set it up. Midway through the installation process, he found a few steps confusing and the manual's screen illustrations didn't match the printer he was installing. Frustrated after trying a few workarounds, he called the support line (faithfully remaining "incognito").

After enduring 20 minutes on hold, the support representative answering the phone informed him that "everyone always calls at this step" because the manual was outdated. Then, the representative shared with him which department was at fault because "they are a mess with shabby quality control".

After receiving instructions, the CEO completed the installation and attempted to run a test print. At this point, all of the lights on the front panel started flashing in unison. Tolerating yet another 20 minutes on hold for support, the next representative insisted that this issue never happens with this printer, and that he must have done something wrong when installing it. The CEO was now forced to recount his every step.

Finally, after defending his own basic skills and abilities, the CEO was informed that this would need to be reported to engineering and that there was nothing they could do at this time!

Still troubleshooting, the CEO decided to search for an answer online. This revealed that numerous customers were suffering the exact same issue, couldn't get anywhere with support, and that the lights have continued to flash since they owned this product.

After this fiasco, the CEO and all executives fully backed the customer experience improvement efforts!

Others have used similar techniques, such as allowing their top executives to serve a day on the front line, or to include them in customer interviewing. Look for your own creative ways to get your point across to top leadership that they need to take the helm in guiding the changes needed. Just be prepared – *executives tend to want to fix any issues they uncover "immediately", so be ready to take action!*

Some votes are easier to get

Many employees will be much easier to steer in the correct direction than others. In a recent meeting, where customer experience concepts were being introduced, several employees chimed back loudly, "It's about time!"

Not surprisingly, these employees were part of the service team. Working directly with the company's customers in their time of need, they already knew these individuals were the heart of their business. This group made it very clear, in fact, that they wanted a program like this for some time. And that they needed support from their executive team, as well as the rest of the organization, much sooner!

Are your employees connected?

On the flip side of the coin, some employees don't have an emotional connection with customers. For example, "far-line" employees (versus front-line), may never speak or deal with a customer. This fact may make it hard for them to "get" this new concept. They may not understand how their actions impact customers at all. It might be difficult for them to comprehend what they need to do in order to put "customers first". Someone in the mailroom may feel that their part is too small to contribute. The computer operator may feel too "behind the scenes" to be involved.

Your project teams may feel that knowing and caring about customers is the responsibility of the "stakeholders".

Employees such as these may be a hard sell, but they are the most important employees to convince. Because they are, most likely, the biggest core and influencers of your company's culture.

Connect the dots for them!

Being a customer-centric organization involves all employees in all departments. Consider this your greatest opportunity to be creative! No matter how "far away from the customer" employees think they are, in fact they are only separated by a few steps. Every employee is an important link in the customer chain. Each link is joined together and counts.

Help your employee identify with customers

Customers may be a vague concept and impersonal facts to many of your employees. But you hold the keys to change this. One great way to help employees form stronger connections is by using "personas".

Personas are easy and fun to create. Turn your archetypes into people (see Chapter 3, "R = Reality Check" for an in-depth explanation of archetypes). Humanize your data by putting faces on them. Dry information transforms into personalities your employees can empathize with. Personas allow them to care about your customers' wants and needs. What better way to connect the dots?

Customer Experience Persona

] 3 - 5
] 9 - 12

Customer Experience Persona

Name:

Age:

Status: [ ] Married   [ ] Single
       [ ] Divorced   [ ] Other
Education:
     [ ] High school
     [ ] College   [ ] Other

Customer since:

My occupation:

My skills:

e, because:

Experience:

What I like the best:

d:

What makes me frustrated:

out your product:

Questions I have:

A quote from me:

Host a Persona Workshop and have employees provide each profile a photo, name, age, and comments to indicate their lifestyle. Describe customer's motivation to buy your productions and their attitude towards your industry. Include a quote that they may say about a service you offer or another applicable subject. Append additional information as relevant to your products and services.

To get you started on the road to creating your own personas, see Chapter 10, "The R.A.V.I.N.G. Customer Toolkit" for several Customer Experience Persona templates. Customize these templates and start using them right away! Most likely, you'll create several to represent different types of customers – men, women, young, old, income brackets, jobs, etc.

Integrate personas into all projects

Make sure that your customers are integrated into your company every day – infuse personas into all project meetings and planning sessions.

Refer to them by name to reinforce a true relationship. For example, when working on a product, say, "I wonder if *Betty* would feel this is easy to use?" Or, if your product would be used while someone works on their car, you might ask, "Can *George* unscrew this lid with grease on his hands?" Empathizing with George could cause your project team to decide to use a tab-top can!

Get your project managers on board by including them as gatekeepers to the persona library. Help them facilitate "Persona Workshops", where they get the project team together to create the personas that they will use. In summary, personas are strategic tools that serve many purposes. They help employees focus on the customer, connect the dots for those who don't have direct contact, and they personify and bring purpose, and a face, to your data.

Ideas to help employees feel closer to customers

■ **Persona workshop** – Bring your arts and crafts skills to these creative workshops. Employees select photos and bring customer profiles to life. See Chapter 3. "R = Reality Check", for an explanation of customer typing and personas, and Chapter 10. "The R.A.V.I.N.G. Customer Toolkit", for Customer Experience Persona templates. Then, take these templates up a notch by creating full persona cutouts, paper dolls, or other creative expressions.

■ **A day in the life of your customer** – Help everyone understand your customers better by illustrating their daily routines. Set up a conference room with several tables to display their lifestyle and the various times your customers interact with your company (touchpoints).

Break through "silo" mentality by drawing out the entire "customer connection" chain. Include an interactive suggestion board, where employees can pin up their own ideas to improve the life of customers.

■ **My customer's journey** – Bring rolls of butcher paper, markers, sticky notes, tape, and other supplies, and have project team members work together to chart out the journey of their customers. Make sure they identify as many touchpoints that they can. As a wrap-up, have them explain how their projects fit within these touchpoints and what they're doing to ensure a cohesive and delightful experience.

- **Our customer workflow** – Host fun sessions in which employees create collages illustrating their own internal workflows. Have them chart each from beginning to end, making sure they conclude at a customer touchpoint. The best one wins a prize!

- **Customer role play** – During these sessions, have employees don their "customer hats" to experience various touchpoints. Include as much of the journey as possible, such as web interfaces, phone messages, emails, and support. Make it a fun game!

- **Customer visit tag along** – Hold raffles where winning employees get to tag along with your front-line employees, as they visit and work with customers. Not only will they feel more connected with customers, they'll gain more knowledge about your organization.

  Publish photos, videos and stories on your company intranet for all employees to enjoy.

- **Connect the dots contest** – Invite departmental teams to create fun posters showing the trail from their department to customers. Have them identify three items or actions that impact customers, originating from their department. The most creative wins!

Be creative – find ways to help employees get involved. Illustrate to them how their role impacts their customers.

To get the vote from all employees, help them understand and feel the customer connection. Everyone needs to feel important in their connection and empowered to make a difference for customers. Executives and staff alike need to feel essential and act with passion.

Give your employees the opportunity to be "hands-on". Involve them in creative workshops, have them draw journeys, engage them with arts and crafts to assemble personas, hold a "connect the dots" contest to show the path from their department to customers. See the previous chart for more ideas.

Also, check out Chapter 8, "G = Get Feedback", to learn about the Voice of the Customers programs and additional employee engagement strategies. Then, visit Chapter 10, "The R.A.V.I.N.G. Customer Toolkit", for Employee Posters and several Award templates.

Can't get everyone on board? Target opportunities based on the importance to your customers, your strategy, return on innovation, and impact to your organization.

Pick your battles

In the game of politics, you may not get everyone united to vote for change in your first time around. This means you may need to select a few easy wins to gain momentum. Be sure to include a high-ranking leader to champion the cause. As pointed out earlier, change can be hard. You may (will) experience resistance.

Just remember, when you are victorious, celebrate all of the employees who made it possible. Even if they were on the opposing side. (Yes, the enemies.) You'll want and need them on your side the next time!

Take baby steps

If you're finding it hard to achieve company alignment, don't give up. Try concentrating in one important area of your organization, and then take baby steps.

There are many advantages to this line of attack. You can find out what works at your company and what doesn't. You can focus on making a positive impact to a high-profile part of your organization. One success can build other successes. And, your executive sponsor will look like a hero.

It may be just the approach you need to get wider buy-in!

Key takeaways:

- Take care of politics and get your leaders aligned with customer experience.

- This is a cultural shift that involves everyone in your company.

- You may have to connect-the-dots to help employees understand their impact on customer's experiences.

- Sometimes, starting with baby steps allows you to make giant strides!

Chapter 6

I = Innovate in Unexpected Ways

Exceptional customer experiences are one of the few brand differentiators that are still hard to imitate. To encourage and cultivate raving customers, you want to provide outstanding experiences that set your company apart and leave an indelible impression.

Good enough is not good enough anymore

In order to raise the bar and achieve the WOW factor, your innovations must go above and beyond expectations. This may sound like a broken record, but this bears repeating. Your customers aren't wowed by "good

enough" experiences that just "meet" their expectations. Being "good enough" won't give you a competitive edge. To have a growing, thriving business, you need to have customers come back time and time again. They need to spread the good word about your company.

To foster customers like these, raving customers, you must do more! You need to provide innovation experiences that exceed their expectations and delight their senses.

Customer expectations are evolving – fast

If the experiences you provide your customers aren't continually innovative, you may find yourself playing catch-up while falling further behind. A great friend of mine in the consulting business tells a story about her own changing expectations to help characterize this situation. Her work often involves travel, and she explains that a few years ago, it was a great convenience to stay at a certain hotel that offered a "business office". The hotel was a bit out of the way, but you could use their computers and printer whenever you wanted, during regular business hours.

The other hotels in the area didn't offer this service, which gave this hotel the competitive edge that attracted many business travelers.

Now, a few years later, business traveler's expectations have certainly changed! Today, hotels are offering free Wi-Fi services so that you can use your own device, tablet, laptop, or other, in the privacy of your own room. My friend points out she wouldn't even dream of staying at this hotel now, which still offers the same old "business office" type of service. After all, who wants to get out of their robe and slippers, get dressed, and go all the way down to the lobby to use someone else's computer? What if you traipsed all the way down there to find the business office closed because it's after "business hours"?

What was once a WOW factor and differentiator just a few years ago is now considered an inconvenience!

Today, who would feel that this was a luxury? Because this hotel didn't continue to exceed their customer's expectations, they have lost their competitive edge and many of their customers.

Customers have learned to expect more

Let's face it, successful customer experience companies have taught their customers, actually *your customers*, to constantly expect better and better experiences. Although you may not be in direct competition with these companies, their offerings have affected your customers. They regularly raise the bar. For example, easy and intuitive interfaces, fast transactions, plug-and-play products, and 24/7 services, used to WOW customers. Now considered standard, without this level of service, you might not stay in business long.

By innovating and providing exceptionally awesome experiences, you'll surprise, delight and engage your customers, and keep them coming back.

Innovation methods

Customer Experience innovations come in a variety of ways, but overall they tend to fall into three categories (and are often a combination of all three):

- **Improved process** – reduction in steps, faster delivery, and smoother workflow. When you improve a process for your customer, you do more than help them complete a task or a series of tasks. You're improving their outlook on what they're doing, as well as getting them back to their lifestyle faster.

- **Made easier** – more intuitive, clearer to understand, simplified steps, and reduced confusion. Remember that your customers don't want overly complicated or sophisticated tasks. They should not have to become experts in order to use your service, product, or interface. Keep it simple and your customers will be happier!

- **More delightful** – added value, more surprising (in a good way), emotionally elating, remarkably better than competition. This is the category where you WOW your customers. Once the top two categories are checked off the list, you can begin to create experiences to impress and knock their socks off!

No matter which of these categories your innovations fall under (maybe all three), you'll want to understand what your customers expect and how to exceed those expectations. Be sure to check the competition as well as the top customer experience companies, who offer similar interactions but aren't necessarily in your business space.

For example, when we started a project to improve our phone messaging system, we wanted to provide a great experience. To prepare ourselves, we sampled the phone systems of our top competitors. These would help us understand our customer's expectations. But, we didn't stop there. We also called companies that we considered the best-in-class, although their business wasn't the same as ours at all. We sampled Apple, Disneyland, Amazon, Verizon, and others.

Check similar experiences offered by the best-in-class companies, not just your direct competition. Then innovate to leave your competition in the dust.

Whether you're improving a process, making something easier, or adding delight, it can be a challenge to raise a "good experience" to a "great experience". But, even though companies have different products, services and offerings, one thing holds true for all – customers like to feel special. The following are a few examples to help you get your ideas flowing!

Idea #1 – Making the romance last

If you can create journeys for your customers that make them feel special at the beginning, middle and end, throughout the entire journey, then everyone wins!

So, it stands to reason that you would want to relentlessly pursue ideas to help your customers feel special. Interestingly, most companies spend a lot of money doing just this before customers actually become consumers. A disproportionate amount of the budget is spent romancing and luring new prospects into becoming new customers. They make sure that is a

delightful time, one that's full of glossy brochures, razzle-dazzle and alluring promises.

It's like a first date with your customers, complete with roses and fine dining. It's all about making them feel special so that they are "bought-in emotionally", and they make the buy!

The problem is, once the purchase is made, prospective clients become ordinary customers. After they sign on the dotted line, there's an invisible hand-off from marketing to operations and support. Here's the kicker for your customers – the level of experiences that these functions provide are radically different.

One day, everything is flowers and champagne. The next, the hard reality sets in and all the thrills are gone. Sadly, they are now *"just another customer"*.

In raving customer experience terms, the marketing and sales period is only a tiny fraction, in fact the smallest part, of the overall romantic journey your customer should have with your company!

The Happy R.A.V.I.N.G. Customers! approach

Imagine giving each touchpoint of your customer's journey the same attention that's given to seducing new customers! To grow raving customers, step back and examine your customer's entire journey from a marketing perspective.

Consider charming your customer at every touchpoint. When it comes to providing these types of exceptional experiences, marketing teams have

long known the value and the competitive edge of the emotional sale in converting prospects into customers. This same methodology is very effective when applied throughout the entire journey.

The whole customer experience lifecycle of your raving customer is important; there are many opportunities for marketing to help make lasting impressions by raising the bar with branded glamour and glitz. Once you can convince your marketing team to see the initial customer experience as a continuum of a bigger journey, they will begin to understand why it only makes sense to continue the romance beyond the dating stage.

Set your marketing folks down with the maps you created during Chapter 3, "R = Reality Check", illustrating your customer's journeys. Get them in a room to run brainstorming sessions. Allow them to do what they do so well – delight the senses with their creative genius.

Turn your "regular customers" into loyal, raving customers by heightening their emotions and making them feel special.

Idea #2 – Say thank you at every opportunity

How wonderful it is to hear the words "Thank you!" We can never get enough of this kind and gracious term. So, why don't we say it more often to our customers? Sure, we may say thanks when they buy something, when they sign on the dotted line. But, when examining your customer's entire journey with your company, how often do YOU say it?

Consider spreading the word of "thanks" throughout each touchpoint. For example, when working with one company, this question forced us to rethink how we were going to approach shortening an "on-boarding" process for new B2B customers.

The existing process consisted of initial meetings and lunches, several back and forth emails and communications, messages of encouragement, multiple visits to their company, getting them to sign the contracts, training them on the offerings, and then several communications and follow-up visits urging them to sell the products and meet production sales goals. The final part of the on-boarding process was declared when the customer achieved their first sales milestone, nine months to one full year later.

After charting this lengthy journey, we asked customers what could be improved. They explained that messages were vague and confusing. They desired a single point of contact instead of three or four different people calling them. They wanted to know exactly where they were in the process and what steps would happen next. Also, since they could be in the same process with multiple companies, they were often confused as to which company's email they were reading.

These customers identified good things too. There were certain "star employees" who were outstanding. They did a better job in providing clear communications. They took the time to build better, closer relationships. They made these customers feel special.

We brainstormed with the marketing team on ideas to help innovate the experience. Our goals were to make it "delightful", streamline the process, help the customer become successful much faster, and to incorporate the "star employee" magic. Everyone agreed; it would be a huge win if we could make all customers feel special throughout the entire process.

The vision: Make customers feel special by providing a uniquely different experience.

That's when it hit us – why not use a series of colorful "Thank You" cards with messages for every stage of the process, and informative websites that matched? It was a bit quirky for a B2B company, but sounded like great fun if we could pull it off.

The results were amazing. Dozens of brightly colored ECards were developed, each containing clear communications that "thanked" the customer and reinforced "how wonderful they were doing". They held links to relevant online information. The ECards were fun, interactive, engaging, and a differentiator.

These customers became raving customers – we received a great deal of positive feedback and "buzz".

Ideas to help with your own innovations

- Chart the journey of your customers, then look at each touchpoint for ways to raise the bar. Begin by making sure that the entire journey, across all channels, presents unified branding, messaging and cohesiveness. Then, move on to add uniqueness.

- Go to the source and ask your customers what would delight them at each touchpoint. Find out what it would take to raise their experience to a level "10". Write down all ideas, even if they are unattainable. Every idea is important and might be useful later.

- When you use customer's ideas, credit them. For example, if you've added something that was requested to your website, append a small credit – "This idea was submitted by." Send a note of thanks with a link so that they can see their idea in action!

- Get in a room with your marketing group. Hold brainstorming sessions to get their creative juices flowing. Go through each touchpoint and show them your customer's ideas. Ask them to think of each point as a marketing opportunity to attract and capture new customers.

- Host similar brainstorming sessions with your front-line employees, who often field suggestions from customers but have no way to voice them. Let them know to "think out of the box, no holds barred".

You might start these sessions with the statement: "If you could wave a magic wand to make it so, what would you do?" Even though many suggestions may be impractical, it's the *suggestion of impossibilities* that often makes us *inventors of fantastic capabilities.*

- Don't forget all channels when looking for opportunities; check interactions across emails, snail mails, websites, call centers, printed materials, etc.

- Find ways to simplify your customer's experiences by shortening their processes, eliminating unnecessary or outdated steps, improving phone messages, and removing unnecessary content on web pages.

- Look for opportunities to jazz things up a little. Involve your graphic designers! This can set you apart from your competition, especially if you're in a traditionally conservative industry.

- Help your loyal customers feel special at every touchpoint. Include coupons, local discounts, tip sheets, helpful references that pertain to their industry, or by adding other values.

- Email fun, branded thank you cards. Send them out after certain stages, such as contacting your support line (Thank you for letting us help you!), making a purchase

(Thank you for your purchase!), completing a survey (Thank you for helping us improve!), or even if you haven't heard from them in a while (Thank you – we hope you come back soon!).

Keep messages simple so that your customers know you are genuinely thanking them – not trying to sell them something.

- Snail mail branded thank you cards. Have the entire team sign thank you cards to send out at milestones, such as larger purchases, anniversary as a customer, or for sending a reference your way.

- To make a customer feel extra special, when shipping their purchase, include something personal, such as a photo of the team wrapping it up and thank you signatures from everyone.

- Create a customer loyalty program. Provide an exclusive service, "in-crowd" specials, renewal discounts, or other offers that help your returning customers continue to feel special and "privileged".

- Encourage recommendations and testimonials by creating a point program to reward raving customers who say great things about your company to others.

- Consider revising the "voice" of your company to a uplifting, casual, fun personality. Use this same upbeat voice throughout all messages and content. Talk to your customers as though they're your best friends, not just acquaintances.

- Ask loyal customers to be guest contributors on your company social media site or blog. This can help grow your raving customer base. It can also be beneficial for B2B businesses, where your business customers have advice to share. This, in turn, helps them to establish themselves as experts in their field and to sell your products.

- Celebrate B2B partnerships. Engage and involve them as often as possible. Provide co-branding services on your collateral, highlight partnerships during presentations to their customers, host informative webinars to their clients and include them on the panel.

- Map the customer experience journey of your main competitors. Compare their journeys with yours to look for differences and gaps in experiences. For each section of the journey, identify the "best in class". Note specific characteristics that set these experiences apart, such as overall impression, emotional response, tone of voice, workflow, accessibility of support, excellence in service, branding, etc.

  Now, go back to your own "journey drawing board" and take this opportunity to design a journey that goes above and beyond your competition!

Making your customer feel special by providing delightful experiences helps build engagement, stronger relationships, and creates an emotional connection that builds loyalty. And, it helps keep your customers away from your competitor's doorstep.

Measuring the return on your innovations

The return on your innovations can be measured in a variety of ways; from satisfaction surveys, customer feedback, and more. You can also measure the *monetary gain or savings* resulting from your customer experience innovations. However, it's good to remember that customer experience improvements equate to more than just gain in time, resources and money. Customer experience improvements *innovate your brand*, and that can be hard to fully quantify.

If you need to show "ROI" at your company, you might use a technique that combines the initial costs applied against internal savings, plus the increased sales and the implications of customer loyalty and brand image.

You may be able to solicit help from your marketing team again. They may know the dollar value associated with attaining new customers versus retaining existing customers, and these figures can be applied towards cost saving calculations. Marketing may also be able to assist with customer satisfaction scoring and other ways to measure brand loyalty as an impact from improved customer experiences.

Internal cost savings from innovation

If your innovation improved a process, there may be a positive impact on your own internal operation and you may be able to quantify a savings.

For example, in the previous "Thank You ECards" story, there was a lengthy on-boarding process that was shortened dramatically. This caused a tremendous internal cost reduction. Originally, the process would involve about 48 hours of an employee's time, spent romancing the customer, writing communications, visiting the company, conducting training, and working with customers to meet sales goals.

Time is money, and this type of information can be used to create a simple baseline expense calculation.

$$\begin{array}{rl}
\$75 & \text{full-burden / hour employee} \\
\times\ 48 & \text{est. hrs each customer} \\
\hline
\$3,600 & \text{cost per customer} \\
\times\ 400 & \text{\# customers 1st year} \\
\hline
\$1,440,000 & \text{cost 1st year}
\end{array}$$

By the end of this project, the on-boarding process was shortened to three months, and the employee's effort to five hours. Using the same calculations, you can arrive at a "rough" improvement savings.

$$\begin{array}{rl}
\$75 & \text{full-burden / hour employee} \\
\times\ 5 & \text{est. hrs each customer} \\
\hline
\$375 & \text{cost per customer} \\
\times\ 400 & \text{\# customers 1st year} \\
\hline
\$150,000 & \text{cost 1st year}
\end{array}$$

Apply this new figure against the original cost and you'll arrive at the estimated annual cost savings.

$$\begin{array}{rl}
\$1,440,000 & \text{original cost} \\
-\ \$150,000 & \text{new cost} \\
\hline
\$1,290,000 & \text{Savings!!!}
\end{array}$$

What we didn't include that the customer is now meeting sales goals in 1/3 the time frame. This means a production increase could also be added to the estimate. Also, this figure doesn't take into consideration that several customers will drop out during the on-boarding process, which would lead to a larger initial customer cost, thereby additional savings. (As pointed out, this is a rough calculation.)

Another consideration is that most of the saving is in "soft cost" – not literally "dollars on the table". The employees are still working and earning their salaries. But, it does mean is that they're freed up to do other things, such as on-board additional customers, and invest more time in relationship building and sales goals.

Eventually, we were able to add in the additional gains resulting from a 32% increase in overall sales for the year!

Hidden costs can start small and add up fast!

Sometimes, when improving customer experiences, there are opportunities to help eliminate "hidden costs". In this next example, I'm reminded that data doesn't always tell the whole story.

Recently, when working with a team to improve their customer's experiences, we collected the company's call center data along with customer feedback. To gather a more complete story, we decided to perform a workplace observation in the call center. This technique, in which someone sits with a support representative to observe them as they answer calls, can help you uncover hidden details.

Before the day's observations began, the support representative was asked, "If we were to fix one issue, which one do you feel is the top priority for your customers?" The rep quickly identified a fairly complex problem she felt was a top concern, because it was a big effort to resolve. She elaborated, "Lots of customers call with this issue. It takes a lot of my time and they're impatient. It's a bad situation all around."

This response didn't agree with our call data or feedback findings. During the day's observation, customers called in quite frequently with a secondary, minor issue that was quickly handled. By the observer's count, customers called with this same small issue 16 times.

Here's where the data was incomplete – this minor annoyance never made it to the call log. Due to the fact that it would take "longer to log it than to fix it", the support representative ended the call and went directly on to help the next customer. This was an accepted practice with small issues as there was no easy way to capture these type of items quickly.

We found some major issues to target for improvements that day. But, I thought it would be interesting if we examined this one, very small problem. Since these types of items are often overlooked completely, this exercise might be insightful. Let's start from the customer's viewpoint.

16 unhappy customers experienced this issue and called in to get help from a support rep. There were 17 support reps. If we assume that all 17 reps received approximately the same amount of calls, this means a possible 272 unhappy customers experienced this issue daily.

$$
\begin{array}{r}
16 \quad \text{unhappy customers} \\
\times \ 17 \quad \text{support reps} \\
\hline
272 \quad \text{unhappy customers / day}
\end{array}
$$

When the phone logs were reviewed, we identified the "average wait time" was just over 2 minutes. Through observation, we knew the amount of time the support rep actually took on the call, which consisted of the initial greeting, the customer explaining the issue, the support rep supplying a solution, making sure the customer understood the steps to follow, and in many cases, waiting for the customer to apply the steps, and then the polite closing of the call.

All of these facts compound this one small issue. For example, if customers were "paid employees", our 272 unhappy customers, after spending just four minutes on the phone with this issue, over time, could cost us a small fortune!

Good thing customers don't charge for their time. Or do they?

The cost impact is to your company's lack of customer satisfaction, loyalty, lower retention rates, and, ultimately, your brand image.

There's more to this story. Let's continue our calculations by connecting the internal, hidden costs of the 17 support reps' time for this one small issue.

$$
\begin{array}{ll}
2.4 & \text{mins. on call} \\
\times\ 272 & \text{\# calls} \\
\hline
652.8 & \text{total mins / day} \\
\div\ 60 & \text{convert to hour} \\
\hline
10.88 & \text{man-hrs / day} \\
\times\ \$55 & \text{full-burden employee} \\
\hline
\$598.40 & \text{daily cost} \\
\times\ 7 & \text{weekly} \\
\hline
\$4,188.8 & \text{weekly cost} \\
\times\ 52 & \text{weeks / year} \\
\hline
\$217,817.60 & \text{annual cost}
\end{array}
$$

The company could save over $217,817.60 in man hours annually! By simply providing an improved experience, they could eliminate the need for customers to call for this small issue in the first place. Then, with the amount of time saved, they could lower the "average call wait time" and concentrate on delivering better support and excellence in customer service. *That's a great return on innovating customer experience.*

Keep innovating

With the help of your customers, marketing team, front-line employees, and others in your company, finding exciting and unique ways to innovate customer experiences is fun and rewarding. Look for ways to surprise and delight your customers.

When you find the right combination and create a breakthrough experience, all of your hard work is worth it.

Then, the experience becomes your differentiator and helps you grow your raving customer base!

Key takeaways

- Exceed customer's expectations for loyal, raving customers.

- The entire customer experience lifecycle of your customers should be romantic, not just the acquisition phase.

- Involve marketing to help continue dazzling and engaging customers.

- Go beyond your competition to create memorable experiences of differentiation.

- Estimate your own "return on innovation" to show the real impact of poor experiences.

Chapter 7

N = Note Success

Y ou've charted your customer's journeys, created your customer experience strategy and plans, gotten employees on-board to vote to change, started on the long road to becoming more customer-centric, and begun innovating customer experiences. Time to take a deep breath – whew!

Now, it's essential to take a moment and celebrate the successes your company has already accomplished. No matter how large or small your successes have been, celebrating helps to reinforce changes, provide encouragement to continue, promote a healthier employee culture, and grow successes.

Reinforce your customer-centric culture

As stated earlier, in Chapter 5, "V = Vote to Change", to be a successful customer experience company and to develop raving customers, your entire organization needs to become customer-focused. Since this can be a major cultural shift, celebrating success is even more important!

Change can be hard to accomplish and many companies struggle with their efforts to become a more customer-centric organization. Part of this struggle is due to the fact that employees need to actively practice their new behavior of focusing on customers, for it to become their standard mode of operation. This means that all employees, across all departments in your company, will need time and plenty of training, encouragement, and reinforcement for this change to take hold, establish roots, grow and flourish.

Often, employees are very comfortable in their current cultural state. Similar to not wanting to throw away an old, worn pair of comfortable

shoes, they can be resistant to stepping into a new, customer-centric culture. Add to this that companies often have micro-cultures and operate in silos; the entire effort can take years to implement.

Measuring the right stuff

Many successful companies, who have turned their operations around relatively quickly, have learned the shortest route between two points is a straight line – the line directly to the pocket book! They see a strong connection between performance rewards and changes in behaviors.

In fact, what you measure and reward your employees for speaks volumes about your company!

To make the most of your customer experience strategy, be sure that you reward your employees for customer focus and for doing the right thing by your customers, and continue to grow your customer-centric culture.

For example, if you reward employees for profitability and nothing else, this will be undeniably demonstrated in your employee culture. They will only care about the next dollar – and that may be the one they're putting in their own pocket, not yours!

In contrast, if you reward for great customer experiences, excellence in customer service, and for the concern and focus on the customer, you will see this reflected in your company's culture and your happy, raving customer base! This, in turn, will ultimately impact your profit growth and retention goals for your company.

Ideas and rewards to help get you started in celebrating success

Whatever you do, ensure that the celebration of your employee's success is clearly linked to their improved customer focused behavior. Design programs, team activities, and awards that put your customer at the center.

All programs should help your staff understand how their achievements are connected to the customer. And, you will be reinforcing to your employees that the company is committed to helping them achieve this new direction.

Customer-centric program ideas

- **Create a "Customer Connection Committee".** Pull together a group of creative employees to form an activities committee. Have them create fun activities to involve your entire organization in learning more about your customers. Encourage an activity at least once a month to ensure the topic stays fresh.

- **Plan a "Customer Experience Personas" contest.** Invite employees to get together in groups to create Customer Experience Persona posters. Give them information about customers or let them investigate on their own. Hang these in highly visible locations for the week. At the end, have your top executives and leaders vote on several "bests" to win – Best Information, Most Creative, Best Emotional Representation, etc. Incorporate your personas in every project.

  If you don't use personas yet, this can get everyone started! See Chapter 10, "The R.A.V.I.N.G. Customer Toolkit", for the Customer Experience Persona Template.

- **Hold a "Front Line Day" raffle.** Employees enter a raffle to win a day with the front-line team (sales representatives, marketing group, and others who have direct contact with customers). Lucky winners have the opportunity to help out and learn more about your most important clients.

Be sure that they can participate, not just observe. Take photos of the day and write articles for your internal Intranet and blogs to keep the buzz alive.

- **Conduct "Customer Dream Journeys" Workshops.** During this fun, hands-on workshop, employees chart out what they think would be a fantastic, magical customer experience journey for your customers. Remind them that this is from the "outside looking in" and to bring their creativity. No knowledge of internal systems needed.

  You never know what might magically appear from this exercise. Supply rolls of white butcher paper, crayons and markers, and watch excellent ideas fly!

- **Create an "I Make a Difference" program.** Punctuate moments when individuals make a difference in the life of your customers. Whenever a customer sends in a positive testimonial, memorialize it on a poster-size print titled "I Make a Difference". Include a photo of the employee associated with the comment.

  Make sure to include your "far-line" employees. For example, if a customer raved about a new billing statement, include the person in the billing department and the programmer.

  See Chapter 10, "The R.A.V.I.N.G. Customer Toolkit", I Make a Difference poster ideas for inspiration.

The link between great customer experiences and employee reward is a key component for cultural change.

Rewarding the right stuff

Everyone loves to be recognized for a job well done. However, many times we end up rewarding employees for doing a job based on criteria that has little to do with our customer. For example, getting projects rolled out on schedule or on budget, or with appropriate functionality. Sometimes, we lose focus on our customer altogether and settle for a less than satisfactory experience – *much less.*

Make sure that your award programs are clearly customer-centric and allow equal participation for your entire employee base.

Customer-focused award ideas

- **Customer Experience "Extra Mile" Award.** This award goes to employees who have gone "above and beyond" to provide extraordinary experiences to customers (directly or indirectly). Ordinary "good experiences", or for what is regularly expected as part of their job, don't apply. This is one where they went out of their way, on their own time, to go the extra mile.

- **Customer "Patent" Award.** Request all employees to contribute ideas to help raise customers awareness or to make customer experiences better. If their idea is selected to be put into action, the employee is awarded a "Patent Number" for their "invention". Post all patents as small brass plaques in a prominent entry area, similar to displays in large, engineering companies.

- **"Caught You Doing Right" Award.** Provide managers several monetary gift cards ($10 - $25) to have on hand. If an employee does an outstanding job in customer service or in improving an experience, they are immediately rewarded on-the-spot.

  To go one step further, have the gift cards themed and specially wrapped. Include a small certificate to display.

- **"RAVING Customer" Award.** Employees win this award because of a customer "rave". Collect customer testimonials of praise from any source, such as emails, letters, blogs, social media, third party, phone messages, etc. Identify all of the employees who are associated with the review, even if remotely involved. If a customer raves about a product enhancement, connect everyone to it, even the person who shipped it.

Make this award something fun and crazy that is a little more interactive. For example, have a crazy, colorful jacket that they put on and have their photo taken. One company even has a straitjacket that they use for their "Raving Lunatic" Award!

Awards don't have to cost an arm and a leg

Connecting employee awards, recognitions, and team-building activities to excellent customer experiences and service is highly effective. Money awards are great, but not always necessary to be successful and contain value. Remember that there are many ways to express "thanks" and to reinforce employees for great, customer-focused behavior.

In fact, sometimes, a crazy photo in a funny jacket, as mentioned above, can be just as effective as a nicely printed, frame-able certificate that contains a sincere thanks and wet signature from your President or CEO. And, neither of these needs to cost much at all.

Making a big impression

I recently met with a manager in her office who had several framed certificates on her wall. Most were the typical, official looking diplomas.

I spotted a brightly cartooned "Thank You", obviously hand-drawn, at the head of her conference table. This looked quite out of place, located in a prominent area of respect.

When I asked her about it, she reported that it was her favorite "certificate" of all. She was awarded this after one of their top customers raved about her in a meeting. The President, COO of the company, and the customer, drew this "certificate" together, and it was signed by all three.

To her, this was a gift from the heart. It demonstrated that she was appreciated for her hard work by the highest people at her company, as well as her most important customer.

Key takeaways:

- Take the time to celebrate successes.

- Cultural change doesn't happen overnight, it takes hard work and practice.

- There is a strong connection between performance rewards and behavioral change.

- Be sure rewards are for doing the right thing for your customers.

- Activities and awards don't have to cost a huge amount to make a huge impact.

Chapter 8

G = Get Feedback

Successful customer experience companies listen to their customers. They listen continuously. They make certain to "bring the voice" of the customer inside, so that it becomes a part of their organization. By hearing this feedback, employees learn and understand their customers' needs, wants and changing expectations. Take a cue from these successful companies – listen to your customers!

If I had a nickel for every time I've attended project meetings and heard someone defend a poor decision by simply stating, "this is what the internal stakeholder wants," I'd be quite rich by now. Clearly, this is not listening to the customer! To develop raving customers, you need to hear what they are saying and LISTEN. The most successful customer

experience companies have made listening to customers an art form. They've set up their own "listening posts" as part of their "Voice of the Customer" (VOC) efforts, and so can you!

Start with small VOC programs and grow in areas that are the most successful for your own company.

Listening from the "inside"

Sometimes you don't have to go far to find out you have everything you need at your fingertips! Check with your front-line employees. They often know exactly what your customers are saying; they hear it every day. The problem is that, quite often, there's not an easy way for these employees to act as advocates for your customers. Don't miss out on this golden

opportunity to collect this information! It's easily attainable and available immediately.

Idea #1 – Set up a Customer Advocacy Board

Creating a Customer Advocacy Board is a great place to initiate your listening prowess and is a powerful idea for setting up an inside listening post. This select team should consist of front-line (or near-line) employees throughout your organization, working together in representing your customer's voice. These board members will act as a major driving force for advocating your customers during customer experience improvements across silos in your company. Because of this, your Customer Advocacy Board will be one of your most politically persuasive tools in your arsenal.

Their mission – *to collect feedback and invoke change.*

Your Customer Advocacy Board will need significant political weight to be successful. You'll want to ensure that their efforts are as trouble-free and uncomplicated as possible. Make sure the right executive is the "owner" of this team and to remove any roadblocks. Kick off the first meeting by having your President or CEO introduce its importance to your company's strategy.

This team's duties won't stop at the monthly meetings. These passionate individuals will be encouraged to identify critical issues (opportunities) when, and as, they come up. To double their effectiveness, make it a hard-fast rule that an Advocate is present to represent your customers in all project meetings.

Idea #2 - Check your support desk

Collecting all call data from your support teams seems like an obvious step in listening to your customer. Yet, I'm amazed at how often this isn't done, or that this data isn't even made available! All information such as this is an opportunity for trending and improvements. Be sure that the data you receive is qualitative (contains actual content, such as what the caller said and the issues being raised). These subjects and issues will help provide insight into difficult and confusing touchpoints. Request phone system data also; the wait times, drop rates, and any other type of information you can retrieve, will be extremely insightful.

Conduct workplace observations to ensure you get the full picture! Be diligent in order to collect even the smallest items that come in. Another important thing to consider – you can use trending data to show gains when improvements are implemented. See Chapter 6, "I = Innovate In Unexpected Ways", for examples on calculating return on innovations.

Idea # 3 - Use outside listening posts

There are numerous ways to listen to your customers from the outside – and more are being created everyday! The traditional venues are still available; surveys, focus groups, and the like, but now there are more and more ways to "eavesdrop" on conversations.

- **Surveys.** As mentioned during Chapter 3, "R = Reality Check", there are many surveys available to gain customer feedback. Be prepared to take action on what you learn. Each question should be connected to an improvement goal or Key Performance Indicator. Always include a comment section! This is where you'll get your best qualitative information. Ask for their suggestions to make this experience a "10".

- **Online instant feedback.** Setup instant feedback mechanisms for your online experiences. Several packages are available, and some linger unobtrusively in the corner of the browser window, to allow customers to provide feedback at multiple points or whenever they feel like it. Customers today are very savvy to this type of feedback method and can be incredibly forthcoming about giving you the straight scoop.

- **Social Media.** Your customers are probably talking about you right now – are you listening? If you don't have your "ears on" social media today, you are losing out (and your competitors are gaining on your naivety). Twitter, Facebook, LinkedIn, blogs. How lucky we are to be able to capitalize on the power of social media! Don't you dare think that social media is only for teenagers – the fastest growing demographic, according to a recent study by Facebook, is age 35 and older.

Chances are, many of your customers are on some type of social media site right now, as you read this book. Do you know if they are talking about your company, your services, and your people? And if so, what they are saying?

Remember, surveys, feedback and other means of automated listening, don't replace the *real conversation* you need to have with your customers.

Maximizing the power of feedback

Be it a complaint or suggestion, it is a wonderful customer indeed who invests their own time to improve your organization. You'll want to grow your staff's appreciation of all customer feedback.

Think of every comment that you receive as a present! After all, this is priceless information.

Yet, many companies fail to maximize on feedback due to their own culture. Often, employees are rewarded for the appearance of maintaining a status quo of "no complaints". If this is your company, then suggestions or issues provided by your customers will be buried, and their value will fly out the window. (This, by the way, would totally stonewall your efforts to become a customer-focused organization.)

Ideas to maximize feedback

- **Integrate all data across all channels.** Combine data to get a holistic view of customer feedback from multiple sources, in order to understand the full impact on your brand.

- **Identify what you want to know.** This will help you develop your research methods and collection strategies based on your desired outcome.

- **Focus on your target group.** Concentrate your beginning efforts on the customers that matter most to your business and will provide you the highest return on your investment.

- **Watch for trends.** As you collect structured and unstructured feedback, look for ways to organize both that allow you to cross compare and uncover trends. This will help you prioritize your efforts.

- **Utilize live feedback methods.** Employ an online monitoring system that allows you to be alerted during failed transactions. For example, a customer aborts a process and a support representatives immediately reaches out to the customer to learn and help with the problem.

- **Distribute good and bad feedback internally.** Make sure that all of your employees know what your customers are saying, not just one or two departments or stakeholders. The best customer experience improvements will come from all employees actively listening and the resulting operational teamwork across your organization.

- **Host feedback sessions.** Hold workshops to discuss the latest feedback. Gather employees into teams and task them to brainstorm improvement ideas. Be sure to include the good feedback too – this provides insight into what customers like.

- **Employ a personal follow-up program.** Close the loop with customers whenever possible. Ask their perspectives on the issues. Let them know that you're committed to partnering with them to resolve problems they're experiencing.

- **Engage customers in real conversations.** Don't "marketize" your conversation – keep it real and honest. Say you're sorry when appropriate and mean it. Then show customers you are willing to do something to rectify the situation – and fix it.

- **Assign "Client Insight Managers".** When negative feedback is collected, assign an employee to the customer, so there is one point of contact. Give them the authority to focus on and correct the problem. This individual acts as the liaison for the customer and follows the case to a successful completion. Allow them to go "above and beyond" whenever possible.

To be a customer-centric company, you need to listen to negative feedback. This is the only way your organization can continue to improve.

Content over quantity

Be careful how you measure customer feedback. Don't just count up how many or how few complaints come in, or what score you achieved. Read the actual comments. If you simply measure the number, you'll miss out on the best part – listening to what your customers are actually telling you!

We'd love to hear your thoughts

How easy is it for your customers to supply feedback? This should be incredibly effortless. Have your Customer Advocacy Board get involved to ensure a straightforward flow of feedback via all channels, including phone, email, and online.

Today, customers expect feedback to be a streamlined process. If it isn't, they'll take their complaints elsewhere – to the streets (social media, of course).

A few months ago I worked with a company who prided themselves on being very accessible to customers. During an interview with one of their sales representatives, he told me that customers were finding it hard to submit a comment on the website. I visited the site, used the contact form, noted that this was a test, and asked for a quick response. I got nothing back. After a few days, with still no reply, I requested that their IT group put a trace on the form.

It was soon discovered that it was being emailed to someone who no longer worked at the company. It was a "dead letter" form!

Be sure that you're easy to contact for complaints, suggestions, and feedback. Don't forget to instruct all employees on the correct procedure when contacted. For example, if they receive an email from a customer via a contact form on the web, they know to reply immediately that the comment was received and is being reviewed. Consider having another procedure for the "wrap around"; after the comment is received and reviewed, if possible, email the customer back and update them on what will occur. And, always thank your customers for the time they took to make their comment!

Listening to your customer is the heart and soul of a customer-centric organization.

If you're not doing it already, start listening today. Your customers are having important conversations and influencing others. *Find out which water cooler they're hanging out at and listen in!*

Key takeaways:

- There's no excuse – there are many ways to collect the voice of your customer.

- Involve your employees, they can collect information and advocate for your customer.

- Feedback is a gift from your customers. Read every comment.

- Listen, listen, listen – and then act!

Chapter 9

Your RAVING Customer Challenge

As I open one of my favorite customer experience books (I measure my favorites by the number of colorful sticky-notes projecting out from the sides that mark incredibly insightful sections), I see the author signed it, "To a fellow customer experience Zealot! So glad you're here!"

At the time she inked this tongue-in-cheek message, I understood the term "Zealot" to be a compliment, defined as "I'm full of zeal about customer experience!" But in looking back at his inscription, I was just a bit curious. So I looked it up on dictionary.com:

- **zealot:** A person who shows zeal. An excessively zealous person; fanatic.

- **Zealot (initial capital letter):** A member of a radical, warlike, ardently patriotic group of Jews in Judea, particularly prominent from a.d. 69 to 81, advocating the violent overthrow of Roman rule and vigorously resisting the efforts of the Romans and their supporters to heathenize the Jews.

With this new awareness, it doesn't escape me that my friend capitalized the first letter! In a way, to be successful in this field of Customer Experience and to develop and grow happy, raving customers, you must not only be a zealot, but a true "Zealot".

You must be ardent and patriotic to your cause. You need to consistently advocate your customers, even in the face of resistance. You must be vigilant. And, I say this with the sword of Customer Experience in hand, ready to do battle!

Are you a Zealot?

In this fight to become a customer experience company and to foster a customer-centric organization, you must battle with a winner's heart.

Your RAVING Customer challenges

1 Challenge the commitment of your leadership.

Gain at least one top executive's buy-in from the beginning. Get their vote, or at least grab their interest. Educate them, buy them books (a gift of this book would be a great start), and invite them to seminars. Make sure they are as interested and knowledgeable in the subject as you are.

2 Challenge the commitment of your organization.

Are they "for" or "against" your customers? You'll learn this by listening carefully during meetings, from statements about the customer and decisions made on their behalf (or not), as well as the condition of your customer relations. Can they change – will they change?

3 Ask yourself, "What is YOUR commitment?"

This effort is not for the faint of heart, and, to be clear, it's not a short-term effort. You must be committed to continue and strive to make a difference for your customers. It may take years, but when you do "move the mountain" – it's definitely worth it!

Sometimes, you'll feel that serving this role isn't pretty. Sometimes you'll win and sometimes you'll fail. But, for every failure you encounter, there will be a success to celebrate!

Whatever you do, don't give up! You must have passion to expect and earn passionate action. As time goes on, if you're extremely pragmatic, you will have many victories to rejoice in!

Astound your customers everyday with a raving customer experience!

Remember:

- **Establish where you are before you begin.** The "R = Reality Check" isn't a long chapter by accident. This step lays the groundwork for all others. It's essential to know your starting point so that you can plot your path to success.

- **Customer experience excellence comes from within – it emanates from your employees.** Follow the R.A.V.I.N.G. Customer Process. Spend time in the "A = Align with strategy" chapter, to work the concepts into the everyday work life of your employees. Utilize ideas from the "V = Vote to change" chapter, and connect the dots for your employees. Be sure to pay extra attention to the "N = Note Success" chapter, which is essential to reinforce the changes in your company's culture – and it's fun.

- **Customer experience isn't owned by a single person or department of your company, it's owned by everyone.** It's not an initiative, or a project, with a start and end date. It's the whole of your organization. Education is crucial; the more your organization knows and understands about customer experience, the larger the impact you'll see in projects, services, and daily operations.

- **Customer experience strategy must be an essential ingredient of your business strategy.** It needs to be embedded, engulfed, immersed, and ingrained in your company culture to be effective. It should describe the way your carry out your business. From the President to the Mailroom Assistant, General Manager to the Line Staff, Venue Owner to the Ticket Handler, everyone must live it and breathe it. Without your customer experience strategy being the heart and soul of your organization, any attempt to encourage your employees to become more customer-centric can end up sounding like radio static. Don't let your customer experience strategy become background noise!

- **Utilize The R.A.V.I.N.G. Customer Toolkit.** See Chapter 10 for your own toolkit to use and customize. Use the Customer Experience Persona Template to build a foundation of personas for your company. Take advantage of the Customer Experience Journey Map Details guide to dig into the details surrounding each touchpoint your customers experience. Create a big-picture snapshot of your customer's end-to-end experiences using the High-Level Customer Experience Journey Map and communicate your findings. Don't forget to celebrate success; use the "I Make a Difference" Poster Templates to showcase employee's making a difference for your customers.

- **Use the R.A.V.I.N.G. Customers Checklist.** Reference this list in Chapter 10 to help you work through your own efforts to create raving customers at your company.

Raise the bar for your raving customers!

I challenge you to romance your customers so that they return again and again! Tell them "thank you" and continue to make them feel special throughout their journeys with your company. Keep the buzz alive. Provide them with exceptional experience to surprise, awe them, make the jump for joy, and knock their socks off!

To grow your own happy raving customer base, give them the WOW factor – they deserve it!

Chapter 10

The
R.A.V.I.N.G.
Customer
Toolkit

After teaching a great group of students at California State University Fullerton, a young man came up and thanked me for providing this toolkit. He pointed out that, not only was he going to modify it for his own company's purposes (as I encourage everyone to do), he was planning to use it toward building his "portfolio". He thanked me for this "gift" that would make him more valuable as he sought out his career advancement. What a nice comment!

That's why I'm presenting this toolkit to you. I hope it will save you hours in having to invent your own portfolio, as well as provide you a jumping off point in raising the bar for your company.

The R.A.V.I.N.G. Customer Toolkit Contents

- Journey mapping – collecting the details
- Illustrating high level journey maps
- Hosting a journey workshop
- Creating customer experience personas
- Employee achievement certificates
- Motivational posters
- Spotlighting your employees
- Your R.A.V.I.N.G. Customers checklist

Download your own full-color PDF version of this toolkit!
www.happyRAVINGcustomers.com/reader-toolkit

Journey mapping – collecting the details

Journey Maps are extremely important in helping you understand what your customers are experiencing. See Chapter 3, "R = Reality Check", where journey mapping is covered in detail.

You may be mapping the entire lifecycle of your customer or just a small part of it, such as the sales or support cycle. Besides capturing current customer experiences, journeys maps are also used to design and innovate *new experiences*.

It all starts with the initial interviews and the collection of details for each touchpoint. The following Journey Map Details template was developed to help your team gather information, in order to start them off on the right foot. Fill each touchpoint out and string them together in order to see the entire journey map!

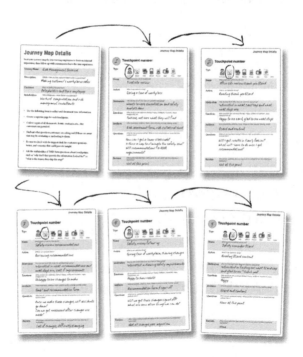

Journey Map Details

Start your journey map by interviewing employees to form an internal impression, then follow up with customers to learn the true experience.

Journey Name

Description   What is this journey about? What is the experience?

Customer   Who is taking this journey?

Stakeholders   Who influences / owns these touchpoints?

- Use the following form to collect and document your information.

- Create a separate page for each touchpoint.

- Collect copies of all documents, forms, contracts, etc., that customers are provided.

- Find out what questions customers are asking and if there are areas that may be confusing or misleading to them.

- Be sure to check with the support desk for customer questions, issues, and concerns that could provide insight.

- Ask the stakeholders if THEY have questions about touchpoints, such as "why don't they provide the information I asked for?" or "what is the reason they skip this step?"

Journey Map Details

 Touchpoint number

Type

In person   Email   Web   Mobile   Phone   Mail   Print   Other

Name — *What would you call this touchpoint?*

Action — *What is our customer doing?*

Motivation — *Why are they here? Why would they keep going to the next point?*

Emotions — *What emotions are customers feeling? Happy, indifferent, frustrated, angry, disappointed, etc.*

Artifacts — *What documents, collateral, forms, videos are they viewing, reading, using?*

Questions — *What are our customers asking? What are their uncertainties or issues that may confuse them?*

Barriers — *What keeps customers from moving on to the next point? Are they skipping or regressing?*

Journey Map Details

 Touchpoint number

Type

In person   Email   Web   Mobile   Phone   Mail   Print   Other

Name   *What would you call this touchpoint?*

Action   *What is our customer doing?*

Motivation   *Why are they here? Why would they keep going to the next point?*

Emotions   *What emotions are customers feeling? Happy, indifferent, frustrated, angry, disappointed, etc.*

Artifacts   *What documents, collateral, forms, videos are they viewing, reading, using?*

Questions   *What are our customers asking? What are their uncertainties or issues that may confuse them?*

Barriers   *What keeps customers from moving on to the next point? Are they skipping or regressing?*

Illustrating high-level journey maps

Once you've completed your interviews, compile your findings into a map that illustrates the journey "at a glance". The following high-level template will provide a useful snapshot of customer interactions.

Start with a map showing the internal impression of what customers are experiencing. Then, make a second map after you've talked to customers (and perhaps your front-line teams). This way, you'll be able to clearly identify the differences and gaps between the two journey maps.

See Chapter 3, "R = Reality Check", where Customer Journey Maps are covered in detail. Then, use this high-level journey map as a tool to get everyone in agreement on these top-level interactions.

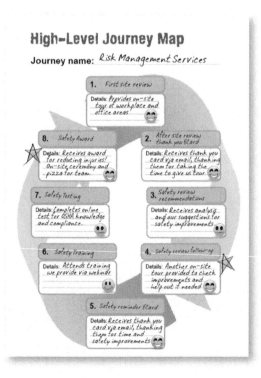

High-Level Journey Map

Journey name:_____

1.

Details:_____

_____

_____

_____

8.

Details:_____

_____

_____

_____

2.

Details:_____

_____

_____

_____

7.

Details:_____

_____

_____

_____

3.

Details:_____

_____

_____

_____

6.

Details:_____

_____

_____

_____

4.

Details:_____

_____

_____

_____

5.

Details:_____

_____

_____

_____

High-Level Journey Map

Journey name:_____

9.

Details:_____

_____

_____

_____

16.

Details:_____

_____

_____

_____

10.

Details:_____

_____

_____

_____

15.

Details:_____

_____

_____

_____

11.

Details:_____

_____

_____

_____

14.

Details:_____

_____

_____

_____

12.

Details:_____

_____

_____

_____

13.

Details:_____

_____

_____

_____

High-Level Journey Map

Journey name:_____

17.

Details:_____
_____
_____
_____

24.

Details:_____
_____
_____
_____

18.

Details:_____
_____
_____
_____

23.

Details:_____
_____
_____
_____

19.

Details:_____
_____
_____
_____

22.

Details:_____
_____
_____
_____

20.

Details:_____
_____
_____
_____

21.

Details:_____
_____
_____
_____

Hosting a journey workshop

Break down silos! Get everyone into one room so that they work together. Have them discuss the journey and each touchpoint. Ask teams to share how they plan to provide consistent, high-quality interactions that work with previous points and subsequent ones.

Be sure to include your front-facing employees who speak to your customers everyday, so that they can provide reality checks to the rest of the group. If possible, invite customers!

Helpful ideas:

- Capture your information on a roll of white butcher paper that can be spread out on a large table.

- Have plenty of sticky notes available in several colors.

- Bring marking pens and highlighters to help people express themselves.

- Use emoticon stamps as a fun way to indicate the emotions the customer may have.

However you do it, the following series of questions will be very helpful in drilling down to the details and getting the conversation flowing!

Journey Workshop Questions

During your workshop session, use these questions as a guide to help spark conversations and to gather information about each point.

1   What type of interface is this?
Example: Web, Phone, site visit, document, email, in-person, etc.

2   What happens now?

3   Is this a "critical" step in the process?
Can it break the journey, buying cycle, stop the process? Can you move to the next point without this one?

4   Why does the customer come to this point?
What is the motivation? What does this step "do" for them?

5   What did the customer do before this?
Where were they coming from? What were they experiencing?

Journey Workshop Questions

6 Does the customer get any service or documents?
Are they referencing anything?

7 What do they usually do next?
Do they ever do something else? What do you want them to do?

8 What happens if someone skips this step?
Is it possible to skip? Will that break anything or leave them without crucial information?

9 Have you heard any feedback from customers about this step?
Are they happy with it? Do they need anything else? Does something confuse them?

10 Have you heard any feedback from internal staff?
Are they happy with the results at this touchpoint?

Journey Workshop Questions

11 Is there any follow up required at this point?
Example: send a communication, supply info, answer questions, etc.

12 What are the questions that customers have at this point?

13 Can I talk to a customer about it?
Or survey? Is there anyone that talks with customers I can speak to?

14 What are the questions that internal staff has at this point?

15 How does this point align with the Brand Values?

Creating customer experience personas

Many companies have data about their customers, but not all companies share that data with their employees throughout their organization. Don't let this happen to you! Put your customers first and help employees understand everything about them. Get teams emotionally connected to your most important assets by translating numbers and unstructured data into humanized personas!

Employ personas in all of your projects, from system development and interface design, to marketing and strategic decisions. To get you started, here are some very simple templates. Create one for each major customer archetype, depending on your business and segmentation. See Chapter 3, "R = Reality Check", and Chapter 5, "V = Vote to Change", for more details.

Sound overwhelming? Begin with baby steps. Create your first personas by asking your front-line employees and others to describe customer types. Once you feel comfortable, grow your competency by doing additional research and adding details that serve your business needs.

Customer Experience Persona

Name:

Age:

Status: [ ] Married   [ ] Single
         [ ] Divorced   [ ] Other
Education:
         [ ] High school
         [ ] College   [ ] Other

Customer since:

My occupation:

My skills:

My experience:

What I like the best:

What makes me frustrated:

Questions I have:

A quote from me:

Customer Experience Persona

Name:

Age:

Status: [ ] Married   [ ] Single
         [ ] Divorced   [ ] Other
Education:
         [ ] High school
         [ ] College   [ ] Other

Customer since:

My occupation:

My skills:

My experience:

What I like the best:

What makes me frustrated:

Questions I have:

A quote from me:

Customer Experience Persona

Name:

Age:

Status: [ ] Married   [ ] Single
         [ ] Divorced   [ ] Other
Education:
         [ ] High school
         [ ] College   [ ] Other

Customer since:

My occupation:

My skills:

My experience:

What I like the best:

What makes me frustrated:

Questions I have:

A quote from me:

Customer Experience Persona

Name:

Age:

Status: [ ] Married   [ ] Single
        [ ] Divorced   [ ] Other
Education:
      [ ] High school
      [ ] College   [ ] Other

Customer since:

My occupation:

My skills:

My experience:

What I like the best:

What makes me frustrated:

Questions I have:

A quote from me:

Customer Experience Persona

Name:

Age:

Grade: [ ] K - 2   [ ] 3 - 5
        [ ] 6 - 8   [ ] 9 - 12

Customer since:

Favorite books:

I enjoy these activities:

My favorite toys:

If I was a superhero, I'd be, because:

What makes me frustrated:

The favorite thing I like about your product:

A quote from me:

Customer Experience Persona

Name: _____

Age: _____

Grade: [ ] K - 2   [ ] 3 - 5
        [ ] 6 - 8   [ ] 9 - 12

Customer since: _____

Favorite books: _____
_____
_____

I enjoy these activities: _____
_____
_____

My favorite toys: _____
_____
_____

If I was a superhero, I'd be, because: _____
_____
_____

What makes me frustrated: _____
_____
_____

The favorite thing I like about your product: _____
_____
_____

A quote from me: _____
_____
_____
_____

Customer Experience Persona

Name:

Age:

Grade: [ ] K - 2   [ ] 3 - 5
         [ ] 6 - 8   [ ] 9 - 12

Customer since:

Favorite books:

I enjoy these activities:

My favorite toys:

If I was a superhero, I'd be, because:

What makes me frustrated:

The favorite thing I like about your product:

A quote from me:

Employee achievement certificates

What's the most important part of your company's journey in becoming customer-focused? Your *employees* and your *company's culture*. This starts from within and there's absolutely no faking it! Guidance, encouragement and reinforcement – essential ingredients for molding your employees into a customer-centric ideology.

Change is hard. Reinforce your employee's success every chance you get!

Punctuate employee milestones with colorful certificates. Be sure they understand the award is for acting and serving on behalf of your customers. Encourage your teams – it's well worth the effort. For more ideas, see Chapter 7, "N = Note Success".

RAVING CUSTOMER

Achievement

Awarded to

_____

Exceeding Customer's Expectations by

_____

_____

_____

Signed _____   **Date** _____

Caught you doing right

For our customers!

Awarded on-the-spot to

_____

Caught you in the act of doing this great thing

_____

_____

_____

Signed _____   Date _____

Customers are RAVING about you!

Awarded to

_____

What customer said

_____

_____

_____

Signed _____   **Date** _____

Motivational posters

Keep the buzz alive – use fun, brightly colored posters everywhere to inspire your employees. Just like inspirational posters, customer-based motivational posters are designed to remind all employees to keep the focus on your customers. Use these throughout your company, posting them in breakrooms, conference rooms and hallways.

Here are some ideas to get your creative juices flowing!

Spotlighting your employees

Build and reinforce your customer-centric culture by shining the spotlight on deserving employees. As mentioned in Chapter 7, "N = Note Success", ensure that the celebration of your employee's success is clearly linked to their improved customer-focused behavior. When a customer presents someone kudos through a testimonial, put the associated employee front and center on their very own poster.

By reinforcing to your employees that the company is committed to helping them achieve this new direction, you can help to shape your company's culture.

Here are a few examples to help you cast your own company "employee star" posters.

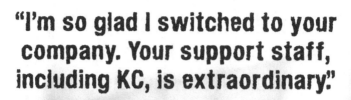

"Jon is an amazing territory manager. He walked me through the entire process. I'm impressed."

– Joe Gardner, customer since 2001

Jon Bean, employee since 1998

I Make a Difference!

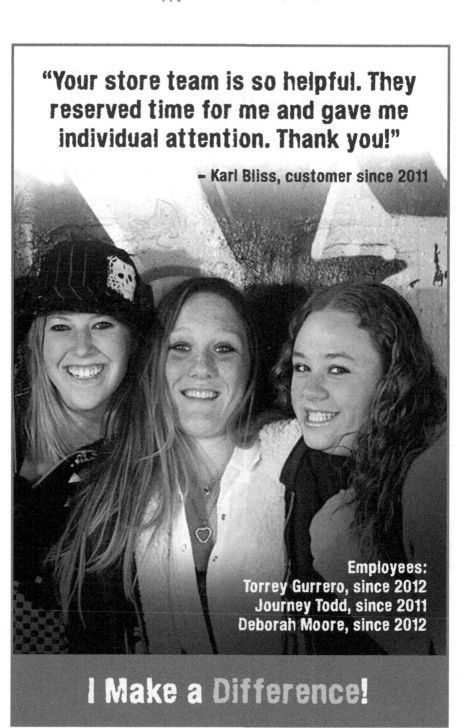

"Nurse Jonnelle is wonderful. She gave us 5-star treatment!"

– Eileen Whitfield, customer since 1993

Jonnelle Franz
employee
since 2004

I Make a Difference!

Your R.A.V.I.N.G. Customers Checklist

This checklist will help you establish your own efforts to create raving customers at your company. As with all items in the toolkit, customize it as needed as you work through the process. Monitor your evolution and improvements as you advance through each of the six steps in the R.A.V.I.N.G. Customers Process. Remember, you may need to cycle through more than once to reach your goals. Keep this list close at hand and check it often!

How many checks you can put in the boxes?

R.A.V.I.N.G. Customers Checklist

R = Reality Check

- ☐ Learn as much as you can about your customers.
- ☐ Collect customer profile data and create archetypes.
- ☐ Map their journey and discover all touchpoints.
- ☐ Find out how your employees feel about customers.

A = Align with Strategy

- ☐ Incorporate customer experience into your business strategy.
- ☐ Create a clear plan of action with goals and objectives.
- ☐ Communicate your customer experience goals to all employees.
- ☐ Educate and help your leaders "lead" your organization in this new direction.

V = Vote to change

- ☐ Start at the top, with your top executives.
- ☐ Work on the cultural shift to be more customer focused.
- ☐ Connect the dots for all employees – illustrate how their role impacts their customers.
- ☐ Take baby steps. Target opportunities based on the importance to your company.

I = Innovate in Unexpected Ways

☐ Look for ways to exceed your customer's expectations.

☐ Make sure you're romancing your customers throughout all phases, not just the acquisition phase.

☐ Involve your marketing team to create dazzling experiences.

☐ Check out your competition, then do something different to create memorable experiences.

☐ Estimate return on innovation to show financial impacts of poor customer experiences.

N = Note Success

☐ Schedule time to celebrate achievements.

☐ Be sure to reinforce positive behavior – cultural change takes hard work.

☐ Establish performance rewards for customer focus.

G = Get Feedback

☐ Create programs and committees to collect the voice of your customers.

☐ To build success, start by listening from the inside, then grow your programs.

☐ Involve employees to advocate for your customers every chance they get.

☐ Use social media – get involved in conversations.

☐ Read all customer comments. Then act!

Key takeaways:

- Use the toolkit and customize it as needed.

- Capture your customers' journeys to understand the experiences they're going through.

- Use personas to help make the customer connection for employees.

- Reinforce customer-focused behavior by rewarding employees plenty and often!

- You'll want to cycle through the R.A.V.I.N.G. Customer Process more than once – it's worth it!

Index

This book was produced using Microsoft Word, CorelDRAW Corel PHOTO-PAINT, Adobe Photoshop, and Adobe InDesign. Photographic images used with permission from Microsoft.

Now, go out and create AMAZING
customer experiences for your own
Happy R.A.V.I.N.G. Customers!

Made in the USA
Las Vegas, NV
09 November 2021